The World is a Book:
Lessons from a Global Odyssey

by
Viney and Kumud Kaushal

Published and printed in
United States Of America

ISBN-13: 978-0-9974448-3-4

ISBN-10: 0-9974448-3-5

Dedication

To Viney's Respected Dad (1925-1996),
keeping a promise made to him in 1993
and
To Vihaan and Arvin, our adorable grandchildren in Boston,
who will carry the learnings further

Contents

Acknowledgements

We still can't believe our memoir is ready for prime time. When we started writing it during the latter part of 2015, we had no idea how much introspection we would need to do to go down memory lane and shake up our subconscious for all the stories in this book. During our life journey of more than six decades, we have met with and befriended hundreds of people from more than three dozen countries. Our sincere thanks to all of them for shaping our journey and giving it a meaningful purpose. This book is compilation of all the experiences we shared with them.

To our respected father, who was the primary reason and motivation for writing this book: we have fulfilled a promise made to him during his visit to Toronto during 1993. May his departed soul rest in peace and his blessings be always showered on us! And our gratitude to all our relatives scattered throughout in India, Canada, USA, and UK for their unflinching support, encouragement, and belief in us.

To our daughter, Megha and son, Varun: you are the best two things that have happened to us. You welcomed us into parenthood. You have weathered many storms along with us as we moved from country to country, uprooting you every few years, leaving your friends behind. You continue to be our biggest critics, as well as admirers. You are the reason we continue to improve ourselves. Thanks for all the suggestions during the writing process and approval of the final product.

To our niece, Bhavna, and her husband, Martin, in Toronto, who spent countless hours going through the whole manuscript and gave many valuable ideas and suggestions for enhancement: thanks will be a mere formality for your love and encouragement.

We would also like to express our gratitude to Kim Kadiyala, Rajeev Gokhale (Abbie, Singapore), Kevin McNeelege and his mom Mary

Teague, and countless others who were magnanimous with their support, encouragement, and constructive suggestions, and who finally saw us through this book.

And how can spouses thank each other? They are soul mates. They understand the feelings of each other even before they are expressed. They have been through this journey together. Each has become part of 'one' in the process. Thanks to the Almighty for uniting us on Earth.

Introduction

"Life isn't about finding yourself. Life is about creating yourself."
George Bernard Shaw

Chicago, April 2016

- This is the journey of Viney and Kumud, a couple who walk the readers through their lives for over six decades as they resided in different places, traveled through various countries, and crossed many cultures.
- They have been risk takers all through their lives and have defied many odds to see the world, feel it, embrace it, and become an integral part of it.
- Even though – or perhaps because - they hold US, Canadian, and Overseas Indian nationalities, they truly consider themselves global citizens with global perspectives.
- These pages are their lives in chronological order; readers prompted to look back at their own lives and reflect on similar experiences will realize how strongly the sequence of events plays a role in our growth and development.

The year is 2016, and we are sitting around our dining table again discussing the next chapter of our lives. We know that out of the 195 countries plus various territories in the world, there are still more than 150 left to explore. The bigger question is how we rediscover ourselves while we continue exploring the world. There are many thoughts and ideas, and we have slowly started implementing them. The ideas range from learning to paint and dance to taking our passion for children's education further. We are also evaluating non-profit organizations where we could contribute, or better still starting our own non-profit for a worthy cause.

We can't underestimate the time we would like to spend with our grandkids. We want to see the world through their eyes as much as we want them to take a few lessons from the lives of their grandparents. If they do, one of the aims of writing this book will have been accomplished. Making sure we do things like this reminds us of how often we are asked whether we have any regrets in life. Indeed, we have many. We can apply logic to recognize that it is not worth brooding over any of them. The journey so far has been fantastic. We want to go at full speed finally without any corporate shackles for Viney. No matter how rational or scientific we are about viewing our regrets, we cannot wholly banish them. However, by going over our experiences through writing this book and sharing what we have learned from those experiences, we can definitively put any regrets behind us and confidently face the future.

We present here our life journey in chronological order. We have divided the book into six chapters, each one describing our experiences in one of the countries in which we have resided: India, Iraq, Saudi Arabia, Canada, USA, and Singapore. Between these chapters, we have inserted ten interludes. Each interlude details our experiences in one or more of the over thirty countries we have visited repeatedly, usually during or adjacent to our time residing in one of the six countries covered by the chapters.

At the end of each chapter and interlude we have summarized lessons learned based on our experiences. These are purely our lessons. As such, we know they reflect how we observe the world with the filters and lenses we have developed that are unique to us now. Readers may have had similar or different experiences, with different people, in the same locations, or in locations we haven't visited yet. We hope our lessons will be equally useful whether you have visited or will visit the countries discussed in this book or never leave the spot where you are reading this now.

Life is a song – sing it
Life is a game – play it
Life is a challenge – meet it
Life is a dream – realize it
Life is a sacrifice – offer it
Life is love – enjoy it

Sai Baba

Our Odyssey

"The world is a book, and those who do not travel
read only one page."
St. Augustine

At the end of the Western Roman Empire, when Augustine of Hippo lived, the lands around the Mediterranean were relatively safe and the roads well-maintained. People traveled as merchants, soldiers, priests, bureaucrats, and pilgrims. The same could be said for many parts of the world then. Although most people were tied to the land they worked agriculturally, visiting other cities, other provinces, was routine. St. Augustine, of course, was writing as a scholar and member of the elite. However, there have always been avenues for people of any means to visit new places. Moving around is one of the things humans do rather frequently. Our species has migrated to every environment on Earth. More often than not, people move because they need or want to find new opportunities. We are two of those people.

Travel provides opportunities of all kinds, the most universal being opportunities to gain new knowledge. Certainly, while reading and hearing about the experiences of others is enjoyable and enlightening, our own firsthand encounters simply cannot be compared. "Being there" has been a primal experience throughout our mutual sojourn. Our knowledge of the world is so much more vivid and memorable than even the most engaging article we have read about any place. However, for people who dream of or prepare for travel, the experiences of others written down or captured in art provide both useful information for future travelers and mind-expanding descriptions of people, places, and cultures for immobile dreamers. Books and other records telling stories about visiting new places extend back to some of the world's oldest texts.

One of the oldest stories still read gave us a name for a long journey in which a traveler learns about himself by experiencing the world: odyssey. This book describes our odyssey. We have written it for several reasons.

- First, we want to tell stories from our lives. The reader will not find out everything there is to know about us, but certainly enough to have a good idea of who we are, what we have experienced, and how we view our world. Whether the reader has known people from India or not, we hope to provide a window into our lives as Punjabi Indians. If nothing else, this book is a record for the generations within our family that follow us to understand the changes we have seen over six event-filled decades.

- Second, the stories provide useful information regarding the places we have lived or visited. Obviously, we spent more time in the six countries where we have lived, and so those chapters are longer. However, sometimes it takes only one event to open the eyes to a different culture.

- Third, we have been enriched by the lessons we have learned as a result of living in many places and traveling to many more. Moslih Eddin Saadi wrote, "A traveler without observation is a bird without wings." The reason behind this thirteenth-century Persian poet's axiom was expressed seven centuries later by an American historian, Miriam Beard: "Travel is more than the seeing of sights; it is a change that goes on, deep and permanent, in the ideas of living." To help others fully obtain these benefits from travel, to be a bird *with* wings, we want to share the lessons we have learned and how we learned them.

- Last and most important, this book fulfills a promise to Viney's father. During his first and last visit with us in Canada in 1993, Viney's father had a special request. One day out of the blue, he started a casual conversation.

"Viney, both of you took a big risk in leaving your comfortable government and bank jobs in India, but I am glad over the years you have proved your decision was right."

I said, "Pitaji [Hindi term of respect for father], risk is a basic ingredient for success in life. If you get stuck in your comfort zone, you can't make any progress. I know nobody could have visualized back in 1981 where we would be or what would have happened ten years after that decision."

"Well, I admit I always doubted the soundness of your decision during the first few years after you both left your jobs in India." Pitaji continued, "I have a special request of you. Will you fulfill it?"

I was quiet for some moments, wondering what the request was. By nature, I always have been nervous about uncertainties. I took a deep breath to gather myself and asked him directly, "What request, Pitaji? You can just command and tell us what you need."

I was surprised by what he said next. "Out of my five sons, you are the most traveled and perhaps best equipped to write a book."

Clearly, he felt comfortable I could fulfill his wish. I was not as certain about my ability. However, he was showing his paternal esteem, and I could not reject his request outright, no matter how I felt.

I asked him, "What would you like the book to be about?"

He replied, "The subject will be of your choosing, but certainly after having traveled around the globe, you and Kumud must have many stories to tell." He said he knew I was capable of creating something that would validate his trust in asking.

I felt overwhelmed by the confidence in me that his request demonstrated. "Yes, Pitaji, I commit to fulfilling your request. One day, I will write a book about the lessons we have learned while living in such diverse cultures like India, the Middle East, Europe, and North America."

Pride, praise, and profit -- the motives behind many books -- are phantoms that may or may not be realized. Keeping one's promise to anyone, especially a parent, far exceeds any other compensation. Viney's father is no longer here to read this book, as he passed away in 1996. Nonetheless, Viney's moral obligation to fulfill his promise remains.

Pitaji recited this Sanskrit sloka [verse] at the time he made his request:

ज्ञानं भारः क्रियां विना

Jnaanam bhaarah kriyaam vinaa
Without action, knowledge is a burden.

In other words, he meant we should spread the knowledge of various cultures we gathered to those who will benefit from it.

Long after Viney's father made his request, we had some time to think about writing a book while in Singapore during a three-year expat assignment from 2010 to 2013. The idea became stronger when we returned to Chicago in late 2013. An early effort to produce something just didn't feel right. However, the desire grew stronger day by day to do something different in life, and the book idea was gaining ground.

Viney worked for Accenture, one of the world's largest IT consulting companies, for the last sixteen years of his career (1999-2015). The company's name is derived from "accent on the future," an apt description not only of the company, but also employees like Viney. As readers will discover, a career can open doors to new experiences and far greater opportunities for learning than can be had at any university. The mundane aspects of doing a job, no matter how interesting, are just work. A career, particularly one that involves moving to new locations, offers far more. As a result, a decision to end a career and go on to do other things must be well thought out. If one has been enjoying success, a decision to follow a different path is bold and a bit unnerving. Yet to do something previously untried, one needs to come out of the comfort zone that feels so warm and safe. One must take risks that endanger one's views of the world, if not one's person or finances. Although we have been taking risks throughout our lives, every decision to strike out in a new direction has brought different unknowns and challenges.

Viney's decision to leave Accenture was made effective March 2015. When we seriously began to think about messages to be shared with people through this book, we discussed the extent that we could offer new perspectives, if not new ideas. Are there any new ideas left? For example, having been an expat is not that unusual for people in many countries. Students do it all the time through study abroad programs. The Schengen Agreement and Eurozone have

4

greatly increased the relocation of employees within the European Union. Globalization has made knowledge of other cultures and sensitivity to differences incredibly important in many business settings. The Internet has eliminated most barriers to finding others who share one's interests. Anyone can be "friends" in the social media sense with individuals living in virtually every country on Earth.

We are not special just because we have lived and traveled widely and know so many people from all corners of the globe. Many people have embraced being global citizens, even people who have never left their hometowns. We certainly know that we became global citizens somewhere along the way. This book describes our world, not just Viney and Kumud's world, but the world everyone inhabits. Everyone, regardless of background or experience, will identify with enough of our odyssey to be able to agree that our story is not exceptional. We are describing the same journey of self-discovery that our readers also take during their lives. However, while not exceptional, our odyssey is, like all others, exclusively ours. Everything we have to offer in these pages is just a different angle of observation.

Speaking of angles of observation, readers will notice that we have tried as much as possible to tell our story jointly. It is *our* story. Please do not be put off or jarred by our referring to "Kumud" and "Viney" as though a third person is describing things. We realized early on how difficult it is for two people to write one memoir. We will try to use first person plural whenever possible. We will try to make clear when just one of us is relating information that only one of us experienced firsthand. Constantly switching back and forth from I meaning "Kumud" to I meaning "Viney" would turn almost the entire book into dialogues with long soliloquies. Maybe our grandkids' generation will come up with male and female versions of first person pronouns. Maybe we will undertake research on what languages do or do not distinguish male first person and female first person and write another book. Until then, our readers must face the challenge of us sometimes referring to one of us by name and with third person singular pronouns being used when one of us is referring to him or herself.

With travel much easier than it has ever been and globalization and the Internet creating many more expatriates, "Where are you from?" gets asked far more often than in the past. That simple, polite inquiry is asked every day all around the world. It is a courtesy to ask a tourist, fellow passenger, or new colleague. It is an icebreaker that opens up avenues for conversation. The reply can be just as simple as the question. Most people are "from" the same place where they were born, raised, and still live. Despite technological advances, people remain in the same general area most of their lives. However, that percentage has been falling. For the increasing number of people like us who do move, the question "Where are you from?" can be more complex. Is it your birthplace? Where you grew up? If your family moved when you were a child, is it the place where you lived longest or completed school? Where you live now?

For example, we are from India. India is quite large – the seventh largest country by area and second largest by population - with many languages, ethnicities, and religions. Still, most people would settle for knowing we are from India. More specifically, we are from Punjab, a northern state of the country that is sometimes spelled Panjab in the Latin alphabet. Although not the case for us, many Punjab residents began living in the new states of Himachal Pradesh and Haryana without moving. Punjab was divided in 1966 to create a Punjabi-speaking majority state, adding Pahari speakers to Himachal Pradesh (a Union Territory at the time) and placing Haryanvi speakers in the completely new state of Haryana.

Punjab is itself divided into districts often named for the largest city in the district. Viney is from Patiala, and Kumud is from Ludhiana, both in the southeast of the state. While Kumud did not move from Ludhiana growing up, Viney moved to various towns because his father was a school principal who often took up different positions in other schools. Certainly in India and places where people know something about India, we would not say we are from India. Depending on the circumstances, we are from southeastern Punjab or Patiala and Ludhiana.

When we lived in Iraq, Saudi Arabia, and Singapore, it would have been silly to tell people we were from those countries. As expats, we were temporary residents. Aside from a small population in Singapore, the citizens of those countries are not descended from immigrants from India. No one would expect us to say we were from any of those countries. Things changed when we obtained landed immigrant status and moved to Canada. We became Canadian citizens. While Indians do not make up a very large part of Canada's population, India is the second largest country of origin among immigrants to Canada. It is not at all odd for someone born in India to say she is from Canada if that is her home. Children born in Canada to parents from India definitely would consider themselves Canadian, just as children of immigrants to the United States say they are Americans.

When we moved to Chicago with the intention of remaining there, it became accurate to say that we are from Chicago. The funny thing is that we can say we are from Chicago, and people all over the world will know about where we are talking; we don't have to say it is in Illinois or the United States. Yet Ludhiana's population would make it the fifth largest city in the USA, and Patiala would be thirty-seventh, larger than well-known places like Atlanta, New Orleans, and Honolulu. We would baffle people outside India if we identified ourselves as from Patiala or Ludhiana, but most people would recognize the names of those smaller American cities. Much the same would happen to people from similar-sized cities in other large countries like China, Indonesia, or Russia. After Moscow and St. Petersburg or Beijing and Shanghai, how many other cities can you name in Russia or China? Indonesia is even tougher. People may know the capital, Jakarta, and nothing else, despite being the fourth largest country in the world by population.

The fact is, hundreds of millions of people are born and raised in places that are not on the map in the minds of others. That lack of knowledge can be a stumbling block for travelers and expats or an opportunity to help others get to know who you are and where you are from in more than the basic sense. State and national citizens are taught quite a bit about their state and nation. Global citizens have even more to learn. Being asked "Where are you from?" gives us the chance to help others identify the parts of the map they don't know. Hopefully, they will retain that information and recognize the place's name in the future.

We have found that it is best to use the other person's frames of reference first when talking about the places we have lived or visited. We will assume our readers have some familiarity with where countries are (if not, world and regional maps are easy to find on the Internet), but we will fill in details around this basic knowledge. After this groundwork has been completed, we can provide more detail and introduce other characteristics that make a place unique and special to us. We encourage everyone to find maps of the individual countries or places within countries to round out our descriptions and give you more to discover on your own. We hope our readers will not only gain a fuller understanding of the world this way, but also will see how they, too, can share their experiences to broaden knowledge and understanding of our world.

Geography isn't the only subject involved in telling our story. History plays a role, too. We moved from India in 1981. It is now thirty-five years later, and a lot has happened in the world in the interim. Additionally, as our readers know, historical events play an enormous role in shaping culture. As similar as they are, we are very aware of how the cultures of the USA and Canada differ. Those differences arose partly from the paths they each took to become independent countries. India gained independence from Britain in 1947 after decades of struggle to convince the powers in London that Indians could manage their own affairs. Britain had been promising the same kind of evolutionary foundation for self-rule as had been applied in Canada. Frustrated by these promises not being fulfilled after India provided immense support to Britain during World War I, comparable to the support Canada provided, opposition to continued British rule grew. However, thanks to the principles enunciated so convincingly by Mohandas K. Gandhi (aka Mahatma Gandhi), India did not experience anything close to the violence of fighting a war of independence. The end process turned out to be rather abrupt and stained by the decision to partition the subcontinent into Hindu India and Muslim Pakistan. The result appeared more like parents kicking a rebellious teenager out of the house.

Indeed, the path to independence for India was not unlike the struggle children face when reaching adulthood, except Indians had thousands of years' experience governing the subcontinent before the British East India Company imposed its rule. Indian parents traditionally have had a great say in the direction their children's lives will take in adulthood. Some might say, particularly in the West, that children should choose their own paths.

If one thinks about it, though, children are greatly influenced by how they are treated by their parents and take their cues in making decisions from how they have been raised. Parental influence is usually very strong and can be backed up with financial support. A girl who does well in mathematics may be encouraged to use that talent to become an engineer. A boy with great musical skill can have parents who refuse to pay for him to attend a conservatory. The extent to which parents decide how their offspring will move into adulthood and the areas in which they exert the strongest pressure varies among cultures. Like almost every society, filial obedience is highly regarded in India. How Indian sons and daughters are expected to express that obedience, however, is different than how offspring express filial duties in other countries.

For example, parents used to decide the career for each of their offspring, guiding their education to the goal they have set, not what the young ones find most interesting. Given the difficulty many teenagers face trying to choose a path once they graduate from secondary school, some relish the idea of being told what to do. Others may find their parents know their interests and talents well enough that the choice made for them is quite suitable. All but the most rebellious children will put in an honest effort to achieve the goals set by their parents, knowing their parents are guided by love and concern for their children's future welfare. Even so, sometimes that effort can fall short of the mark.

Viney was designated to be a medical doctor by his father. Unfortunately, he missed the entrance exam cut-off score by a few points. His father then pointed him toward becoming an Ayurvedic doctor (naturopath). Viney did not want to become one and instead studied biochemistry and management and wound up working for a bank, moving into government, human capital management, total quality management, and then consulting and alliance management. Not becoming a doctor was disappointing to his father, but eventually his father ended up feeling no disappointment in Viney's actual career path. We would not have had the experiences we have had, and Viney's father probably would not have asked him to write a book, if Viney had achieved the goal his father set for him.

9

A common practice around the world for many centuries has been for marriages to be arranged by parents. Marriage is an alliance between two families that had greater significance before many people traveled widely. The union could have political, economic, or social implications, or any combination of these. Dowries and bride prices were transfers of wealth, as were instances in which a daughter inherited property (if the law allowed) that would be controlled by any man she married (if the law allowed). Written stories about relationships based on love go back as far as 2100 BCE, but they rarely involve marriage arising from that love. Couples were expected to grow to love one another or at least tolerate their partners. Even in the late 1970s, arranged marriage was the accepted tradition in India.

We broke with that tradition. Our marriage was not arranged by our parents. We met while working for a bank in Ludhiana. Destiny has played a vital role in our lives. Viney and a colleague were scheduled to be transferred in the bank. The colleague was supposed to go to Ludhiana but wanted to trade assignments with Viney. Viney agreed, and the bank allowed the change.

In mid-1976, we were paired for a special project to visit doctors in Ludhiana and convince them to open deposit accounts with the bank. Obviously, we spent quite a bit of time together each day and got to know each other better. One afternoon after finishing our visits with various doctors, Viney suggested that we go out for soft drinks. Socializing between unrelated members of the opposite sex was uncommon in India at that time, even two work colleagues. Viney had been toying with the idea for the last few weeks if Kumud would become his life partner. It was all one-sided at that point and highly unusual for a man to choose his life partner like this with no parental involvement. During that fateful evening, Viney gathered the courage to propose to Kumud, not knowing what her reaction would be to his question or his break with tradition. She happily accepted the proposal with a caveat. She asked that we give it thought for a few more days before finally committing. Within a few days, we reconfirmed our commitment and thus broke an important tradition of not involving parents in this decision-making process.

Although marrying each other was our choice, we certainly wanted our parents' blessing and acceptance. Kumud's parents came around fairly quickly, but Viney's father spent some energy protesting our union. He felt he had been robbed of a parental right once again, having already had to accept that Viney was not going to become a doctor. After a couple of years trying and hoping to gain his approval, we finally married officially in May 1979 with his reluctant nod. Viney's father still was not on board 100 percent. In fact, it took Viney's father a few more years to put the slight behind him. Eventually, he told us that he had been wrong to object. He graciously and honestly told us that Kumud was a wonderful daughter-in-law. Major credit for his change of mind goes to Kumud; she had proved to him through her behavior since the marriage and in her dealings with him that she was an ideal daughter-in-law.

Although we had not been able to change his view that a father's prerogatives included selecting spouses for his children, he did accept the fact that our different approach had resulted in a very happy outcome. We have seen many times that this is how traditions evolve and cultures adapt over the years. Change is the only permanent condition in the universe. However, change can come at an unacceptable price if we completely ignore traditions. While we have demonstrated our independence by stepping away from some traditions, we remain connected to those traditions. For example, as we will discuss much later, we continue to study and practice Hindu precepts. We are the sum total of the people and culture that preceded us and the new experiences we integrate into that initial framework.

Life is a tapestry that becomes more beautiful as more threads are added. To avoid creating a mess of the work, anything new must be integrated with the old. It is far easier to pursue or accept change that is gradual, like sediments building islands in a delta, than to deal with change that is rapid, like lava and ash erupting from a volcano. In our journey, we have gradually adapted to and adopted change as a result of our experiences. We hope our readers will see the benefits of facing change as the transformation of what exists now rather than as the displacement or destruction of the past or present. We also hope they reflect on changes in themselves that have resulted from their own journeys.

India (1952-81)

*"We live in a wonderful world that is full of
beauty, charm, and adventure.
There is no end to the adventures we can have,
if only we seek them with our eyes open."*
Jawaharlal Nehru

Viney was born in Patiala in September 1952, just five years after India gained its independence from the United Kingdom. Kumud was born less than a year and a half later, in February 1954, in Ludhiana. Viney prefers to spell our home state "Panjab", and Kumud prefers the more standard "Punjab." Despite this difference of opinion (and maybe a few others), we have remained married since May 6, 1979, and raised a daughter (Megha) born in 1980 and a son (Varun) born in 1984 while moving to different countries every few years. Although we have visited India many, many times, we have not lived in India since we were young adults. Still, we were born, raised, and educated in India. We met and married in India. India is the largest part of our story and remains the greater part of our identities. The southeastern part of Panjab/Punjab will always be home, regardless of where we reside. The borders of India surround our hearts.

One thing we have learned in our travels is that children tend to have the same experiences wherever they are raised. A significant factor affecting how their lives differ is economic. Children from less fortunate families are in some ways more similar to one another in different countries than they are to children in wealthy families in their own country. Culture and language, however, result in significant differences even within the same country. Our childhoods would have been much different if we had been raised in Bihar or Kerala or Mumbai. In fact, they would have been different if we had been raised in the north of Punjab instead of the southeastern part of the state.

Still, we have found that even more important than economic status, location, or culture, it is family relationships that mold the shape of our children the most. Caring, responsible parents and grandparents, as well as closeness to siblings, create a nurturing, supportive environment. However, even when a parent is physically or emotionally absent, children can learn positive lessons that will help them in the future. We recall our childhood years and transition to adulthood with great fondness, not because our experiences were universally happy. Our warm memories remind us that we were given a wide range of opportunities to understand the importance of getting the most from life. Here we share our individual memories of growing up.

Viney's Upbringing

I was born in Patiala, a princely town in Punjab that had a rich tradition of being a pioneer in producing fashionable women's clothing, particularly richly embroidered articles. However, in the 1980s, Chandigarh, a newly developed city just thirty miles from Patiala, became a new center for this craft, usurping Patiala's distinction. Unlike many cities in India, Patiala is not very old. The city was established by a Sikh leader and a Muslim leader in the 1720s who built a castle and wall with ten gates to oversee the territories they had joined together. Supposedly, they divided power by making the Sikh founder the first maharaja [king] and the Muslim founder the first army commander. Those roles continued in their families. To this day, Patiala has a royal family whose head even served as chief minister of Punjab's government early in the twenty-first century.

My childhood was modest but interesting. When I was born in 1952, my father was a teacher in Patiala. He had a knack for insisting at work that everything be done his own way. While this attribute can demonstrate strong character and self-assurance, it also can be seen negatively, especially by superiors who want things done their way. My father offended school managements all the time. As a result, he found himself without a job every few years. When I was seven years old, one of these situations arose that turned out to be a blessing in disguise for him. He got a big promotion and moved our family to a large village where he became principal of a school, effectively without any superior management looking over his shoulder. This made him his own boss. Luckily, with him now in a

13

position where he could do everything his way, we did not move when I was in primary and secondary school.

My father was extremely patriotic and a zealot for Indian Hindu values. He had been a very active member of Rashtriya Swayamsevak Sangh (RSS). The RSS was established in 1925 as a Hindu nationalist, non-governmental organization separate from the independence movement. Its members pledge selfless service to India. The RSS had been banned by the British colonial government. It was shaken when a former member assassinated Mahatma Gandhi in 1948, although an official inquiry absolved the organization, its leaders, and its members of any involvement.

The early 1950s were the initial years of India's independence. Our people were still used to applying *Satyagraha,* the principle of nonviolent opposition, for one national issue or the other. Being a passionate activist, my father routinely volunteered to go to jail on behalf of RSS in support of the just side of such issues. I have vivid memories of visiting my father in jail while I was still quite young. He always used to boast of the comforts he received while jailed because he was a university graduate. The British had given special privileges to university graduates sent to their jails, and free India had continued to do so.

I distinctly remember the streets around our maternal home in Patiala. My childhood days were spent playing in the streets with other neighborhood kids, doing naughty stuff around elders, trying to catch loose kites, and visiting the neighborhood temple almost every day to take the sweets and money left as offerings. I still recall an incident when I was only four years old and was exposed to a live electrical wire in our street for an extended period of time and would have died if not saved by some neighbors. We were a group of four or five kids playing hide and seek in the street. No one noticed a live electrical wire in the street corner. I accidentally caught it in my hands. It must have been in my hands for a few minutes. My fingers were burnt. The other kids were quick to shout loudly, getting the attention of neighbors who rescued me. It took many weeks to recover fully. Still to this day, I am not comfortable with electrical gadgets and wiring.

My two older brothers were a big influence on me during those early days. Being the third son, I received no special treatment from my parents the way a first or even second son might. However, when we planned naughty tricks together, my older brothers granted me a certain kind of special treatment. Being the youngest of the lot, and therefore the smallest, I had the proud privilege of being assigned jobs that were too risky for my brothers. I could go undetected in places they could not.

Those days are clearly engraved in my memory. I am grateful that they are. It is quite easy for me to see how things have changed over the decades and how some things remain the same. For example, I still recall my maternal grandmother was very particular that I should not touch scavengers. Scavenging is considered an unclean practice in Hinduism. Back then, scavengers were also called Untouchables because people like my grandmother said they should not be touched. One day, I touched a scavenger accidentally. I was given a bath immediately. Nowadays, we call this group *Dalits*, a word meaning "oppressed" that was chosen by the people formerly called Untouchables.

The caste system in India remains an important part of how people view themselves and others, even though it has evolved to be less rigid. Castes make up a system of social stratification that has ancient origins. According to Hindu scriptures, its origin reaches back thousands of years when Manu, the progenitor of humanity, divided society into four groups or *varnas*:

- *Brahman*: Educators and educated (the highest caste)
- *Khashtriya*: Warriors
- *Vaisyas (Bania)*: Traders/Merchants
- *Shudra*: Laborers

Though these classifications were originally function-based, people gradually made it based on birth. For example, even if a *Brahman* is employed as a trader, he remains a *Brahman*; he is not considered a *Vaisya*.

While the British used the four *varnas* to assign castes to everyone during censuses, Indians traditionally have used the related term *jāti* to identify the community or clan to which they belonged. *Varna* and *jāti* are basically different levels of analysis of the caste system. Just as there are thousands of occupations beyond those ascribed to the *varnas*, there are thousands of *jātis*, one for each occupation. Layered onto that is identification with clans, tribes, and religions. As a result, the caste system has extended beyond its Hindu roots and touches every religious community in India.

As I mentioned earlier, *Dalits* traditionally were considered untouchable and were even considered to be outside the *varna* system. They and other less respected *jātis* were more or less condemned to always be on the lowest rungs of society. The Indian government calls members of the lowest castes "Scheduled Classes" and promotes education and employment through affirmative action programs for them to finally move up socially and economically. In fact, a *Dalit* was elected President of India in 1997. It is a relief to see how much India has changed since my childhood memories were formed.

Kumud and I were born into *Khashtriya* families. While this commonality certainly has helped me and Kumud to understand one another, a more important factor is that we are both middle children. I already mentioned my two older brothers. I also have two younger brothers. We all have been successful in our careers thanks to the strong support we had from our father and the continuing support we have had from our wives. Not only have my four brothers and I led fulfilling lives as professionals, our children have followed in our footsteps.

Krishan, the eldest, was born in 1945 when my mother was only 16 years old. He joined the Indian Army as an officer, serving for twenty years before choosing to retire as a colonel in 1988. He and his family immigrated to Canada in 1994, following in our footsteps. Krishan still actively works in a corporate job despite being past the normal retirement age. He lives in Toronto with his wife. Their three children are professionals: a daughter who is a vice president in the financial sector in Toronto, another daughter who is a medical doctor in Miami, and a son who works for Microsoft in Seattle. At times, Krishan still questions if he made the right choice to move to Canada when he was 50 years old. Such questions are common for most immigrants from time to time. We ventured out of our cultural comfort zones and occasionally wonder if we would have been more contented staying in familiar surroundings.

Vijay, the next oldest, was born in 1948. He completed a B.S. in Agriculture and a master's degree before becoming an officer in the State Bank of India, where he worked for thirty years before retiring in 2008. He is currently chairman of his own education business in Punjab. His two sons are doing well. The older one is in his father's education business. He manages schools in India and Singapore and is now expanding the business into the United States. He is a homeopathy doctor by profession but clearly has the genes for entrepreneurship in his DNA. His wife is an educator. Vijay's second son is a consulting executive with Accenture, my former employer, near Delhi. His U.S.-educated wife is an architect and runs her own business. Vijay lives with his wife, another educator, and their older son's family in Chandigarh. Such arrangements, with families spanning three generations living jointly, are traditional throughout India.

Yoginder, the next after me, was born in 1956. He is an executive with Punjab National Bank. He lives in Mohali, Punjab, with his wife, one of his sons, and the son's family, another joint family arrangement. His second son and his wife live in the U.S. Both of his sons and their spouses are professionals.

Rakesh, the youngest, was born in 1958. He is a homeopathic doctor. He and his wife, who is also a doctor, have a practice near Chandigarh and live there. Their older son is a doctor, and the younger one is completing medical school in Mauritius. Both will carry the family medical profession forward.

Aside from Krishan, my brothers and I each have two children. In total, including our daughter and son, there are eight males and three females in the next generation. The odds are quite good that the Kaushal family name will continue, but now spread among three countries. With three of my brothers living in Chandigarh, our frequent family trips to India bring all the extended family together, a great reunion of sorts. We always look forward to such opportunities, knowing full well life is short.

My mother was highly religious. She always fasted on many auspicious days and visited temples regularly. She was a huge influence on all five of her boys. She inculcated religious values in all of us. I will never forget that fateful day of December 9, 1963, when my mother passed away at 34 years old during the delivery of my sixth brother. It was the darkest day of our lives. My mother's death will always stay as one of the events that changed the personalities of all five of us brothers forever.

Mother was married at the age of 15 and had her first child at the age of 16. By the time she was 33 years old, she had five children, ages 17, 14, 10, 6 and 4. Her pregnancies were spread out, unlike the wives in some large families at that time who were constantly pregnant early in their marriages. I was the ten-year-old. I had two older brothers to look to for support and two younger brothers who needed even more support than I did. We had become motherless at a very young age.

Then, and even now, in India women oversaw all of the housework and almost all of the children's needs. Since we did not have a sister who could help with household chores, managing our household became a big issue. My maternal grandmother came to spend time with us. She lovingly helped us through the critical first six months. Then our father's sister's daughter, who was about 20 years old, came to help for the next year. It was becoming increasingly difficult to manage with limited help like this. This phase made me and my older brothers mature quickly and learn the day-to-day affairs of a household, especially cooking and cleaning. That made us self-sufficient and reliable, traits that helped us through our college days when we stayed in boarding schools.

The oldest son is supposed to take the ashes of a parent to the Ganges. It is said that the night before this duty is completed, the son has a dream in which the deceased speaks to him. Krishan, the eldest among us, went to the Ganges with my mother's ashes. Just as we expected, our mother came to him in a dream. She said, "This was not my turn to go. I should not have gone. I was taken by mistake. I will stay around to watch over my sons."

There is a tradition in India that the mother's younger sister is normally the best candidate to marry her deceased sister's husband and take care of her sister's family. My mother had a younger, eligible sister, but she was already in love with someone and thus could not marry my father. It was sad for my father and us children, but perhaps best for her. However, my father finally married again in 1965. He was 40 years old at that time. We discovered quickly that the transition to having a stepmother would not be completely smooth.

After a month, our new stepmother complained that our mother's soul was in our home. A tantric mystic, like a sorcerer, who invoked the gods by name, was brought to the house. Tantrics go to midnight rituals at cremation grounds to gather powers and knowledge. Even today, people in smaller towns and villages or from less well-educated backgrounds rely on witchcraft to influence relationships like parents wanting to break up their daughter and her boyfriend.

The mystic who came to our house meditated for fifteen minutes and said he talked to my mother's soul. He confirmed she was there, but only to watch over her children. Surprisingly, the mystic knew her name, where she was born, and her father's name. We had never told these details to him. He told my father to give our mother's favorite foods to the poor. It seems my mother had complained to the Tantric that she was not getting her favorite food. And he ordered the soul to stay one mile away from our home. After that, our stepmother never saw the soul again.

Our logical minds question such incidents. Yet, I witnessed the whole ritual of the mystic myself. Reason tells me to wonder how such things are possible but fails to decide whether I should believe in such things or not.

Our stepmother was a good companion for my father. However, we boys did not get the type of love we would have gotten from our birth mother. A part of us never got enough motherly love and affection. We have remained thirsty for that missed bond. Knowing that gap, we brothers ensured our own kids received enough love and affection from both parents. Luckily, none of us has had to face the situation that my father went through after the death of my mother.

I can vividly recall growing up in a rural village. From fourth to tenth grade, I was enrolled at DAV High School, Garhdiwala, Hoshiarpur, in Punjab, where my father was the principal. We lived in the school and owned a cow and a buffalo to provide us with dairy products. One time, I watched the cow give birth. It was a unique experience at my age. Sadly, on another occasion our buffalo was dying. My brother Vijay and I stayed with her and read Chapter 18, the last chapter of the *Bhagavad Gita*, an ancient Hindu text. The chapter summarizes the lessons from the other chapters and promises the attainment of perfection and Nirvana if one surrenders to Lord Krishna. By reading this, we believed we helped the buffalo to either end the cycle of reincarnation or be reincarnated into a superior species, e.g., as a human.

I was responsible for taking the cow to the nearby forest for five hours or so daily for it to feed and fertilize the forest. To pass the time, I always took a few books with me. I read hundreds of books in Hindi and many in English as well during that phase. We had a library in the school that wasn't used by many students. Since I enjoyed reading so much, I was given a key to the library so I could borrow books whenever I wanted. I only had to write the book title on a slip of paper. I miss that period of my life.

One of my favorite activities then (and now) was flying kites. There is something wondrously joyful and relaxing about chasing a kite as it weaves and dips on invisible breezes. As the son of the school principal, however, I was expected to study as often as possible, not fly kites. The times my father caught me, I would receive a thrashing. I got such pleasure if I wasn't caught that even today, whenever we visit India, I make a point of flying a kite, knowing I will not be stopped. Of course, our new home in Chicago, the Windy City, lets me indulge in this activity almost whenever I feel like it, but sadly nobody flies kites here.

I should mention that we are talking about a time when corporal punishment was ubiquitous in most countries. Parents, especially fathers, disciplined their children in many ways. Striking a child in a manner that would cause no permanent physical damage was the norm even in the United States. Indeed, school teachers also enforced discipline with paddles and other measures. It was not unusual for parents to tell teachers to "smack" their sons if they got out of line. School principals in particular were expected to enforce the rules strictly on the theory that corporal punishment had the most vivid effect on teaching children the consequences of misbehaving. Nowadays, psychologists have demonstrated that physical discipline does more harm than good; much of what we experienced is considered abuse now. While we certainly did not enjoy being punished, we always seemed to find reasons to be naughty with the hope we would not be caught.

The village was 18 kilometers from the nearest town. Back then, rural areas did not have toilet facilities of any kind. We would go to the forest with some water to clean up after. Men had no modesty about taking care of things in the open. Women crouched behind trees. Improvements since that time in smaller villages include communal toilets that still require, as in most of Asia, crouching. That aspect of personal hygiene has lagged behind urban areas in which Western-style facilities have become common.

Another problem was that during the rainy season the postal service couldn't reach us because the roads were impassable. We had to wait for weeks at times until the season was over and the roads dried out before we got mail again. Unlike in the United States, where rains and floods rarely last longer than a week, the rainy season is just that: rainy for months. We would watch the water flowing past the school carrying debris as large as furniture and trees.

While the rainy season wasn't much fun due to mud, mosquitoes, snakes, and muggy heat, the period when mangoes ripened was quite enjoyable. Everyone had mango groves. There was a tradition for the parents of students at the school to invite the principal and his family on the weekends for a meal while mangoes were ripe. We kids were allowed to pick fruit for ourselves. We had to be cautious, though. The groves were home to many snakes on the ground, in the trees, and in burrows. We had to be particularly careful about walking around the openings to the burrows in the ground, and even more careful to avoid cobras. Cobras will strike without provocation. Fortunately, we were never bitten. We would take the fruit to soak in water and then suck off the juicy pulp around the big seed.

I finished high school in 1968. Due to my father's constant supervision, making sure I studied, and all of the reading I did, I was top of my class from grades 4 to 10. In grade 10, everyone took standard state level exams. The hard work paid off. I was sixty points ahead of the next student in my class. More importantly, I was first in our district. As a result, I was given a national scholarship through graduation.

Grades 11 and 12 in India were completed at a college in those days. This part of my education was to prepare for medical school admission. In 1968, I attended DAV College in Jullundur. Also known as Jalandhar, Jullundur is the oldest city and was the capital of Punjab before Chandigarh. The reason place names have more than one spelling usually is that linguists change the way non-Latin scripts are converted to the Western alphabet. Sometimes politicians want to change the name from whatever the colonial power called the place. Either the old Romanization scheme was inaccurate or the Europeans who first visited the place misunderstood how the residents were pronouncing the name of where they lived. So, Bombay is now Mumbai, Burma is now Myanmar, and Peking is now Beijing. In Alaska, Mt. McKinley was recently renamed Denali out of respect for the native peoples. Maybe these changes explain why some people find geography a difficult subject.

I lived in a student hostel in Jullundur during grade 11. I had never had such freedom before. I was just like a kite skittering in the air connected to the ground by a thin string. That string was my sense of obligation to satisfy my father's goal for me. While it was strong enough to remain unbroken, I took full advantage of being able to fly about. I particularly enjoyed going to the Bollywood movies. I'm sure I saw every film produced that year.

In 1969, I transferred to Arya College in Ludhiana, which is closer to where my parents lived. Still, I remained unsupervised in my activities while staying in a hostel. I met friends who would sometimes go to the movies with me. They also invited me to go with them on weekends to their home villages and towns. I certainly can't say I was bored while in college. And I did put effort into learning the material I needed for the medical school admission examination. I never got into any trouble that would be reported to my father. He must have been satisfied with my progress, since he was encouraging rather than critical.

In India, medical school begins immediately after grade 12 at institutions specializing in training physicians. Entrance is based on scoring above the cut-off on the entrance exam. I missed admission by only a few points. This was another instance when fate clearly played a role in my life. My score was high enough not to raise any suspicion that I had been fooling around in college. It was low enough that I was saved from fulfilling my father's decision for me to be a medical doctor.

Not to be dissuaded, my father secured my admission to Ayurveda College in Patiala for a five-year program in naturopathy. He desperately wanted me to become a doctor and would be pleased if I succeeded in this alternative path. However, I knew this was an unsuitable path for me after those two years of preparation. I had learned enough, as my exam score indicated, to know becoming any kind of doctor treating illnesses was not in the cards for me. I defied my father and did not join the program. However, I waited until a week before classes began to inform him. I did not want there to be time for him to expend too much energy trying to change my mind. Although he remained displeased with my action for some time, he was realistic enough to know that I had firmly and rationally chosen not to follow the path he had set for me.

Instead of learning naturopathy, I enrolled at Punjab Agriculture University in Ludhiana to obtain a Bachelor of Science degree in Biochemistry. This was a golden period of my education. I truly blossomed as an individual during this period. I met many, many people, some of whom became lifelong friends. I chose wisely. These friends are now acclaimed scientists, professors, bankers, chartered accountants, and Indian Administrative Service officers in high positions. Although I could have continued in science and obtained a master's and PhD in Biochemistry, once done I most likely would have had to search for a university position overseas. Becoming a scientist is not what I wanted to do at that time.

I decided to move to business management. Punjab was the only agriculture university in India that offered an MBA program that focused on the agricultural sector. It was well respected in the industry and, since India was still very much involved in the Green Revolution to increase agricultural yields, employment opportunities were abundant. To be honest, the point of education from my perspective and that of most Indians is to make one attractive in the job market. Also, I was interested in being selected for the Indian Administrative Service (IAS). Taking on managerial positions would give me the opportunity to prepare. What happened after I received my MBA will follow the story of my wife's childhood and education.

Upbringing

... of five children, three sisters and two brothers. Both of my brothers are older than I, and I am the middle child among the sisters. We lived in a joint family that included us children, our parents, and our grandparents. Throughout India, joint families have been common for a very long time. A joint or undivided family is an extended family arrangement consisting, as in my family, of several generations living in the same home. The family is headed by the oldest male, who makes decisions on economic and social matters on behalf of the entire family. All property is held jointly. This system is disintegrating today due to the fact that recent generations hunt for opportunities outside their birthplaces, moving anywhere, whether within India or to foreign countries, to advance their careers. Younger members of families no longer stay in the households in which they were raised nearly as much as they did just a few decades ago.

My mother was a devoted mother and daughter-in-law. Everyone liked and respected her. My father was hardly ever home to participate in our upbringing. He was, in a sense, missing from our lives. Despite a lot of effort on my grandfather's part to set him on the right path, my father never became serious about his responsibilities. Later, this proved to be quite unfortunate. As an only child, my father acquired the investments my grandfather had built, and he squandered them. He could never become a role model that children try to emulate. As a result of my father's absences, I owe my mother and grandparents a great debt for shaping my future and my siblings' futures. They provided the right guidance and means to help us become what we are today.

Having our grandparents living with us was a special blessing. They ended up being a profound influence while we were growing up. In particular, my grandfather served as our philosopher and guide through our years in education. He took an active interest in our school homework, choice of subjects, and career guidance. He ensured financial resources never caused a bottleneck in our progress. He truly filled the void created by our father's unavailability. My grandfather was the patriarch of our joint family. He had earned enough for us in his overseas assignments to lead a

24

comfortable life by investing in large properties. There was enough of everything in the household.

Our grandmother needs a special mention in this regard. She was a devout and serene lady. She began each day with three hours of prayer. She poured love and affection on all of us, which bound us together through her. We owe her a lot for inculcating religious values in us. I am grateful that I have inherited calmness in my life from her. I vividly recall one year when we were celebrating Lohri, the harvest festival celebrated in northern India that also marks the end of the winter season. Our grandmother asked my mom to prepare a traditional sweet dish of rice and sugarcane juice. Once the dish was ready, I was the one who took it to her. Grandmother did not respond to my repeated calls. That is how I realized she was no more. In India, we believe that any death on an auspicious Hindu festival day is sacred and leads to freedom from the bondage of life and death: Nirvana.

Our house was a good size for the number of people who lived in it. The furnishings were not particularly fancy, but they were comfortable and stylish. It was very common for friends and relatives to visit for a week, sometimes even without advance word they were coming. My sisters and I were all taught the basics of cooking. We had a few helpers at home to assist with completing household chores and raising a few cows and buffaloes. We also had a dog called Happy who lived with us for 12 years, a special favorite of my mom.

Girls were educated separately from boys. Although we could be just as naughty as boys, we did not face corporal punishment for misbehaving. If we disobeyed a teacher or did not complete our homework or class assignments, we had to stand in the front of the classroom with our hands over our ears. This was quite embarrassing. Sometimes they might have a girl continually stand up and sit down in place at her desk. I still fondly recall us girls used to go to school in a cart driven by horses. Now in India, it is a thing of the past, and the carts driven by horses have virtually disappeared almost everywhere.

Education for all of us kids was the main emphasis of our mother and grandfather. We grew up understanding that we were going to complete high school and college at least. As it turned out, I studied up through a master's degree without any interruption. In college, I majored in political science and economics. I found the former to be my favorite field of study, so I continued as a political science major in graduate school.

While in college, I had a couple of close friends, but one named Harjit became my best friend. To this day, we are close to each other, and our families are close, too. She even traveled all the way from India to the United States in 2009 to participate in our daughter's wedding. My sisters and I are also very close with one another, more so than with our brothers. I was considered the favorite of my mother out of the five children. She immigrated to Canada with us late in 1993 but stayed for only one year because she missed India. During the last years of her life, after she returned to India, my husband and I took care of her needs until the last moment.

In a nutshell, I grew up in a loving environment, except that I missed my father's love and guidance all along. I was twenty-two years old when I met Viney. He and I dated for two and a half years before we were married in May 1979. The concept of dating was not common in those days. This was perhaps an indication of many events to come in life where Viney and I broke barriers while treading on many unpaved roads.

Our Careers in India

Kumud was a banker all through our working years in India (1975-81), except for a short stint as a lecturer at a college. Kumud joined the Indian Bank in Ludhiana in 1975. She subsequently moved to the bank in Shillong from 1979 onwards because of her husband's transfer to that wonderful region. Some of Kumud's colleagues in the bank became our very close family friends and continue to be so.

Viney's career was more varied and colorful and took many unexpected turns. Viney recounts:

After receiving my MBA, I started working in 1975 in the pharmaceutical industry as a representative for Lupin Labs in Mumbai and Amritsar, selling prescription drugs to doctors for their patients. I worked in this field for six months and left because I did not like my job. I had to wait in clinics for hours just to get a five-minute audience with the doctor. Even then, there was no guarantee the doctor would prescribe the medications produced by the company. Given my earlier experience just barely missing the required score for medical school, this position confirmed that I was not destined to be associated with the medical profession, even remotely.

I started looking for avenues of employment in the banking industry. This turned out to be an intelligent choice. I landed three jobs to be an officer in three different banks, almost simultaneously. I chose to join Indian Bank Chennai. They got preference since theirs was the first offer I received and I was already with them undergoing training when the other offers came. This also turned out to be a fortuitous choice. Little did I know that destiny was conspiring for me to meet someone through this bank, someone who would become my life partner.

Getting a job as an officer with a bank during those years was a big achievement. The position provided lifelong job security, timely promotions, mobility within the country, reasonable salary, and respect in society. The bank had new officers rotate to new assignments for training every six months. My first posting was in Chennai. After that I was moved to Ludhiana, where I had been fortunate enough to meet Kumud, and finally Simla. During my last training leg in Simla, I started thinking of becoming an Indian Administrative Service (IAS) officer. I also started thinking of another career that would give me time to prepare to become an IAS officer. That is how I landed my next job.

In 1977, I became an administrator with the Indian Council of Agricultural Research (ICAR), a part of the Ministry of Agriculture. This turned out to be one of the most enriching jobs I had in India. I was managing the administrative functions for hundreds of agricultural scientists. It was fascinating to see plant research creating hybrid varieties of grains for increased production. This field was critical since India was in the middle of the Green Revolution and was making significant leaps forward creating different high yield varieties of wheat, rice, maize, barley, vegetables, and fruits. The late 1970s was a golden period of Indian agricultural advancements; I was fortunate to witness it firsthand while dealing with research scientists and visiting fields.

In Hyderabad, I was with the rice research institute in Rajendra Nagar. I lived there from July 1977 to December 1979. The city lies in south-central India, almost equidistant from the Arabian Sea and the Gulf of Bengal. The city's current history dates back almost to 1591. It is important partly as the capital of Andhra Pradesh, a state created in 1956 for Telegu and Urdu speakers. Residents of the United States, Canada, and most countries are used to the boundaries between states or provinces being fixed. Not in India. Ethnic, language, and religious communities have many valid reasons to not like being split into different political divisions. Creating Andhra Pradesh addressed some of those reasons for some of the communities. However, others felt less well represented and strove on and off from 1969 to 2013 for further change. Their protests prompted the government to agree finally to create the new state of Telangana from the nine northwestern districts of Andhra Pradesh. At present, Hyderabad, well within Telangana, is the capital of the new state and remains the capital of Andhra Pradesh until that state's government is moved by 2024. The city also hosts the winter offices of the President of India.

Having been associated with the trade in pearls (and gold) for centuries, its nickname is the City of Pearls. In more recent decades, Hyderabad has attracted many research facilities, financial companies, and information technology businesses, both Indian and international. In fact, the city's newest nickname is Cyberabad. A substantial percentage of the population works in the services sector, just as I did so many years ago.

The entire time I was in Hyderabad, Kumud and I did the best we could maintaining a long-distance engagement. I would take the train to Ludhiana every three months, a journey that took one and a half days one way. We were hoping that my father would accept the fact that we became engaged without his input. Of course, I could not tell him that Kumud and I were seeing each other whenever I could get away. Kumud continued to work for the bank where we had met. Eventually, my father agreed to a formal wedding ceremony in which everyone participated, albeit a few reluctantly, in 1979. Kumud, now my wife, moved to Hyderabad as a new bride in May 1979.

We lived outside of Hyderabad and have fond memories of going to town for sumptuous southern Indian food, Bollywood movies, shopping, and meeting friends. We had a two-wheel scooter, a prize possession at that time. I just loved how my wife would sit on the back holding me tightly, lest she fall during the ride into the city center. Of course, it wasn't as much fun when a neighborhood dog who was a favorite of Kumud would chase me down the road. Fortunately, he only got some exercise and never caught up with us.

We were very fortunate to have my older brothers, their wives, and children visit us during this time. We had a splendid time. We used their visit as an excuse to explore Chennai and Bangalore (Bengaluru), two large cities in the southeastern states of Tamil Nadu and Karnataka. We had great fun singing on the train and catching up with one another. I cannot emphasize enough how fulfilling it is to learn firsthand about the diversity within one's homeland.

While those memories are important to us, even more special was that we were living together as newlyweds. As our readers know from their own experiences or observations of friends, those first few months to a year of sharing a home with a spouse create an environment that includes love and anxiety in equal measures. Each partner discovers new quirks and interests, routines and behaviors. Suddenly, your relationship demands greater trust, patience, and forgiveness as both people explore a deeper understanding of the other person in the relationship.

All of this becomes even more intense and complex when the couple begins life together far from their original home without family or friends nearby to help answer the inevitable questions or provide the wisdom of experience. It's like trying a new recipe and deciding to do it blindfolded using your memory of what you think are the ingredients and steps involved. Who knows? If it is a one-pot dish using components that can be identified by touch or smell, you can end up with a very tasty curry or soup (and a very messy kitchen, no doubt). On the other hand, if you try to make an elaborate dessert, well....

We weren't too far along in making our "meal" when a radical change interrupted us. In December 1979, I was promoted to a very challenging senior assignment in Shillong, in the state of

Meghalaya, looking after the administrative needs of scientists in seven northeastern states and union territories. These are commonly known as the Seven Sisters: Arunachal Pradesh, Assam, Manipur, Meghalaya, Mizoram, Nagaland, and Tripura. The area has borders with Bhutan, Bangladesh, China, and Myanmar, and is connected to the rest of India by a narrow corridor of land. During 1962, China invaded inside Indian borders in Arunachal Pradesh. It remains a disputed territory with China. That is why one has to be very careful while traveling. And I had extensive travel to all these states to meet with scientists and administrators.

Unlike in Hyderabad, where the research institute only studied rice, the agriculture research program in the Seven Sisters included work with all kinds of vegetables, fruits, and grains. Humans have been adopting and adapting wild varieties of plants to provide food ever since the very first farmers planted seeds to intentionally grow crops instead of relying on gathering whatever fruits and seeds they could find for their meals. The results are all of the produce and cereals we have today that are larger, sweeter, or healthier than their wild cousins.

The process of creating improved food plants has rocketed since Mendel discovered the difference between dominant and recessive traits in sweet peas. The researchers I assisted administratively, along with over one hundred staff members, carried on that tradition. I helped them set up facilities, handled paperwork and supplies, and provided whatever was needed for them. It was fascinating to see test fields of plants that not long before were just experiments the scientists hoped would lead to success.

Our entire stay in Shillong was highly educational. For example, Shillong is comprised of the Khasi and Garo communities, which are matriarchal. The primary means by which this is enforced is that the youngest daughter inherits the family property unless the parents name an older daughter. Families without daughters choose daughters-in-law or adopt a girl into the family to maintain the matrilineal family. Women were the bread winners and were working in every walk of life in the city, while men played second fiddle to them and mostly played cards and chatted away the day. A few men become employed as police officers and drivers, but their wives still controlled the household. Not too surprisingly, literacy is higher among women than men. However, subsistence agriculture predominates in the rest of Meghalaya. In the mountainous rural areas that make up most of the state, the women own the land as matriarch of the household, but men must perform some of the tasks required to make a farm productive.

There was minimal mobility of local people, with residents rarely straying outside their town. So much so, many of them had never seen a train in their lives; the nearest train station to Shillong is three hours' drive away in Guwahati, a town in Assam. We also saw many children with both north and south Indian features. Given the diversity within India, it should not be surprising that people within one region tend to have physical features that differ from those of people from distant regions. Migration within India typically was rare until modern times. On enquiry, we were told many Army officers and other service people from different parts of the country come to the area for two or three year assignments. They marry local girls during their stay, produce kids, and move on at the end of their assignment. Their local wives never move with them, most likely because women have more authority in the family in Shillong. In many cases, these ladies never see these men again.

When we moved to Shillong in mid-December, the city was under curfew due to local agitation to gain more autonomy for Meghalaya. We were confined to a guest house for one week and could not even go out the door. This small city sits almost one mile above sea level. December is a cold month in that part of India (cold for India, at least) due to this elevation, with lows around 45°F and highs around 60°F. On top of that, while the winter months are quite dry, Shillong receives about 410 inches (34 feet!) of rain each year; the records for most rainfall anywhere in the world for a month and for a year were set in two towns just south of Shillong. We were wondering if we had made a mistake in coming to this troubled, uncomfortable region. Between the chilly air and the confinement, we certainly were not looking forward to staying long enough to experience all of that rain. Little did we know that the next two years were going to be so rewarding, not only from the knowledge about our country that we learned, but on the family front as well.

It turned out that Kumud had become pregnant during our last two months or so in Hyderabad. Our daughter was born in Shillong

31

on July 6, 1980. We gave her the name Megha, from Meghalaya state. Now she is an established business professional in corporate America, but our memory of her early development in Shillong is still as fresh as if it were yesterday. Some of our fond memories include her first birthday in Shillong, her first words, her first steps, and of course, her first use of the alphabet. We are reliving her childhood through our grandkids now.

Since Kumud was working for the bank, we had no option other than to ask my maternal grandmother to live with us and help us raise Megha. Usually, this practice has not been too burdensome because families tended to remain geographically close. It was quite an experience for my grandmother to move almost from the far north of India to the far northeast, 2,200 kilometers from her home in Patiala. She had to get used to significant changes in culture and climate.

After a year, we asked Kumud's mother to take my grandmother's place. Again, we were doing something that was atypical. In Indian culture, a wife becomes part of the husband's family. While the wife continues to cherish her birth family members, Indians believe a wife's mother should not help raise her daughters' children. Symbolically, the husband's mother-in-law is intruding into his family if she becomes involved. While we could understand the reasoning for this tradition, in practice someone had to look after Megha when my grandmother needed to go home. Whenever some family need is met in a traditional way for generations, no one thinks to provide substitutes until enough families face the need and cannot rely on the traditional way. Daycares and nannies were not a common practice at that time, since most people were just following the traditional way of getting childcare assistance from the paternal grandmother.

Our overall experience in northeast India was just fantastic and full of many things to learn. We were able to travel to all seven states and union territories and were exposed to the customs of each of them. While I traveled quite frequently to conduct my work, Kumud was able to accompany me at least once to each of the Seven Sisters. We also managed to visit Sikkim, which is adjacent to Bhutan. Sikkim used to be an independent kingdom that chose to abolish its monarchy and join India in 1975. It has the smallest population of any Indian state, and the second smallest territory (after Goa, a former Portuguese enclave on the Arabian Sea). Bhutan remains independent with a king. Both of these places are renowned for the huge variation in climates, from subtropical to mountains among the Himalayas that reach four miles high, and for their ancient associations with Buddhism.

The northeastern region of India has a special, magical beauty. The hills and valleys are home to hundreds of tribes with many languages. The manner of dress, eating habits, and overall way of life can appear similar, one to the other and distinctive at the same time. The entire region is an ethnic mosaic. Festivals and celebrations in the northeastern states are very colorful, reflections of the people's embrace of life and the closeness of their lives to their unique communities. Each state has its own array of cultures and traditions. For example, Christianity, mostly Presbyterian and Roman Catholic, is by far the majority religion in Meghalaya. However, the Khasis, the state's largest ethnic group, retain many festivals from their traditional religion.

It was particularly interesting to see the varieties of food habits in the region. Throughout most of India people eat chicken, fish if they live near water, and beef if they are Muslim or Christian. However, the people in Nagaland and Mizoram eat snakes and virtually everything else that moves, including snails, rats, squirrels, dogs, cats, buffaloes, deer, spiders, monkeys, red ants, and almost everything that is wild, even including elephants.

While traveling through this area, you feel you are in paradise, with magnificent hills and green meadows filled with thousands of species of flora and fauna. The northeast has a number of wildlife sanctuaries and national parks where rare animals live under government protection. The world famous Kaziranga National Park, a world heritage site, is in Assam. It houses two-thirds of the world's one-horned rhinoceroses. Our family had a great time returning to Assam to visit in 2004 and travel through the park on elephant back.

Speaking of wildlife, one incident that is just engraved in our memories about the region happened in 1981. While Viney lived through the experience, Kumud was almost as profoundly shaken just hearing about it.

As Viney recalls: I was accompanying a senior scientist of the center. We were traveling by jeep in Arunachal Pradesh. It was 10:00 p.m. and our jeep broke down on the road in the middle of the jungle. That jungle is famous for tigers, black bears, and cheetahs. Since there were no means of mobile communication at that time, there was no way to get help. We suddenly realized we were trapped in the middle of animals that could attack us at any time. It was very unlikely anyone else would be using that road that night. The driver of the jeep decided to go to the nearest town on foot six or seven miles away. He told us to switch the headlights of the jeep on and off from time to time to scare animals.

During the next five or six hours, we saw the flashing eyes of a few animals. Presumably they were cheetahs, but the glare of the lights scared them and nothing attacked us while we were stranded. Help finally arrived around 4:00 a.m. Another jeep took us to safety. I must confess this was like a new birth and the most frightening escape of my life. Even today, those piercing, hungry eyes of the cheetahs haunt me from time to time. I can smile at that experience today, fully realizing that this story and this book might have evaporated that fateful night after one jump of a cheetah.

In sharp contrast to that terrifying night, more than anything we remember and cherish the warmth and friendliness of the people we met in Shillong. In Hyderabad, our friends and colleagues sent us off in a raucous, wonderful style. We feel very fortunate that the same experience occurred in Shillong. Over the years, people throughout India have become used to meeting transplants from other areas that will only be staying temporarily. By 1981, Indians were moving around the country quite a bit more than at independence in 1947, although this was in relative terms. Many, many people stayed put and only witnessed migrants like us. With such a large country and such a diverse population, we are grateful to have been among those given the opportunity to experience so many facets of Indian culture.

In November 1981, the Indian Council of Agricultural Research head office asked me to move to Simla as senior administrator of the potato research institute. Simla is a small city that serves as the capital of Himachal Pradesh. The name is pronounced and often spelled "Shimla." Simla was built in the nineteenth century by the

British, eventually becoming the summer capital of the Raj, with a fitting residence for the Viceroy. As a result, much of the architecture is mostly the English Gothic and Tudor styles.

Simla lies about 75 miles northeast of Chandigarh and 130 miles northeast of Ludhiana, close enough to make visiting family much easier, but far enough away that it would be a new experience. While we could consider the move to be another adventure discovering another part of our country, we had a problem. The research institute in Simla focused solely on potatoes. After having been involved, albeit tangentially, with scientists who were investigating the potential of new hybrids of many varieties of plants, the thought of potatoes and only potatoes sounded rather unappetizing.

When I learned of the transfer, we immediately decided we needed a more radical change. To a certain extent, the decision arose from our inability to get anywhere in joining the IAS, which had been the goal for both of us. I asked my older brother to inquire about opportunities in Iraq, where he was stationed by the Indian Army at the time. By the time I moved to Simla, I had secured a position in Iraq. Kumud and Megha moved to her brother's place in Chandigarh while I took a leave of absence and left for Iraq. We had no idea at the time how radical this step was going to be. At the time, it was just another attempt to find advancement opportunities.

We feel very fortunate that not only our stay in Shillong, but all of our time in India has provided us with so many lessons.

- *Scarcity is good.* Although we had enough to fulfill our basic needs, Viney and his brothers were brought up with limited means, as salaries for education staff were meager at that time. We can appreciate what we had and what we have had over the years because we know how thin the line is between getting by and not getting by. Knowing what scarcity is from a young age makes us eager to conserve resources and make the most out of what we have, rather than looking for more.
- *Education is critical.* We would not have met and married, had children, and taken this wondrous journey if we had not obtained the fullest educational opportunities available to us. Indian parents will do anything to ensure their children receive a good education. Western readers will think this is nothing unusual, but

bear in mind that even in parts of the United States and Europe there are parents who do very little to support their children's education. In India, graduates create a foundation for their advancement, just as others do around the world. However, Indian parents see that foundation as a reflection of their determination to see their offspring succeed as much as the determination of their offspring. In a society that has long suppressed social and economic mobility, Indians today know many of the barriers have fallen, and to prove themselves worthy they must pursue education as far as they are able.

- *Extended families are irreplaceable.* Indian families are very close, and many live as a joint family. Pooling resources guards against individuals being harmed by adversity and reversals of fortune. Parents will know that they will be looked after very well in their golden years. Many societies have moved away from living in extended families, shifting some of the burdens of unemployment, illness, and age onto the government and public. While social safety nets can work, they are impersonal and sometimes embarrassing to use. The joint family system ensures each generation does its share, accepts its responsibility, and fulfills its duty to the other generations in the household. This system helped us tremendously after the unfortunate demise of Viney's mother. Authority flows from respect and affection as much as seniority and, as we discovered in Shillong, does not have to be patriarchal.
- *Obstacles bring opportunities.* Bureaucratic red tape is as old as the most ancient civilizations. India is the successor to a long line of empires and kingdoms, plus the British Raj that have each contributed to making red tapism a major religion among government employees. The overall bureaucratic system makes one look for opportunities particularly when, as was the case then and is so again now, opportunities are limited. We found several opportunities when Viney left the bank and started working for the Agriculture Department. He learned to be a human capital administrator. We lived in parts of the country vastly different than Punjab. Our knowledge increased, and we acquired a taste for seeing new places. While Viney's intent was to gain experience in order to join the IAS, we discovered

36

instead that we ought to look outside India, where the opportunities were much greater. The key to this lesson is that when one encounters an obstacle, you can go over the obstacle, around it, or even under it. Regardless of which way one chooses, you will be heading in a new direction with new vistas and new opportunities waiting.

While growing up, we learned the mantra below to be chanted before undertaking any journey, whether spiritually or worldly. The significance of the mantra is it will make the journey successful, peaceful, and enjoyable. This is exactly what we needed before taking the unknown, arduous road ahead in our lives.

*Om tryambakam yajāmahe sugandhim puṣṭi-vardhanam
urvārukam-iva bandhanā mṛtyormukṣīya māmṛitāat*

ओम त्रयम्बकं यजामहे सुगंधिम पुष्टिवर्धनम
उर्वारुकमिव बन्धनात मृत्युर्मुक्षीय मामृतात

Om. We worship the Three-eyed Lord Shiva, Who is fragrant and Who nourishes and nurtures all beings. As the ripened cucumber (with the intervention of the gardener) is freed from its bondage (to the creeper), may He liberate us for the sake of immortality

As is customary, I chanted this mantra three times and started the most interesting journey of my life at the age of 29.

Viney's parents:
Som Prakash Kaushal and Kailash Devi
Garhdiwala, India, 1961

Kumud's Parents:
Dina Nath and Satyawati Sood
Ludhiana, India 1945

Kumud's graduation picture
Ludhiana, India 1974

Viney – NCC Cadet
Garhdiwala, India, 1962

Bridegroom waiting anxiously
for the bride
Viney – Ludhiana 1979

Marriage solemnized
Viney-Kumud
Ludhiana, India, 1979

Kumud with Megha
Iraq, 1982

Viney, Kumud, and Megha
Kashmir 1983

Iraq (1982-85)

*"Everyone without exception believes his own native customs,
and the religion he was brought up in, to be the best."*
Herodotus

Iraq was at war with Iran from 1979-1988. Our stay occurred during the middle years of this conflict. Our experience was so much different than living in the United States during the wars in Iraq and Afghanistan. Aside from whatever was mentioned in the news or whenever one encountered someone whose son or daughter was serving the U.S. military, Americans could easily forget their nation was at war with two countries plus pursuing terrorists in Pakistan, Yemen, and elsewhere. In a smaller, less developed country like Iraq, it was almost impossible not to be reminded of the war every day.

We learned to live with scarcity, the predominant reminder. Key resources were needed for the war effort, depriving consumers of consistent access to many products. There were always shortages of the most basic food items, like vegetables, milk, eggs, and meat in the markets. If we saw a line while driving, we automatically stopped the car and joined it. Only after we had secured a place in the queue would we ask for what everyone was standing in line. Sometimes it was something inessential but nice to have, like sugar, other times it might be something nutritious but pedestrian, like onions or eggs. Reflecting back, it is interesting that sugar, which had been a luxury in pre-modern times, could so easily become a luxury again.

Moving to Iraq was risky for many reasons, not just because the Iran-Iraq War was going on. We made the decision for Viney to try to find employment there because advancement in India would be slow and difficult. We looked to Iraq specifically because Viney's eldest brother Krishan was there. He had been deputed by the Government of India to go to Iraq in 1979. He was a military officer responsible for teaching engineering to Iraqi forces in undergraduate programs. While it may sound odd today to think of governments assisting Saddam Hussein's regime, back then he was an ally of India, the U.S., and other countries that saw Iran as a threat. As it turned out, Krishan found Viney an opportunity that looked very promising. The position was Human Resources Director for TCNs (Third Country Nationals) employed by Dragagges et Travaux Publics, a French construction company with a contract from the Iraqi government to build a road being constructed through Iraq's western territory, from Kuwait north to Turkey.

In December 1981, Viney took a one-month leave from his government posting to Simla to take the job. Now the other risks became apparent. Would Viney want the job once he was there? Would the company want him after he started? What was it going to be like working for Europeans instead of other Indians? Having no experience outside India, would the change in environment and culture be too much to handle? Would he handle the different diet? Was he going to be able to obtain permission from the company to bring his wife and daughter there to live with him? If he did, would we even like living in Iraq?

The only thing that was not really too risky was whether Viney could get his job back at the Potato Research Institute in Simla. Although he had taken only a short leave, we discovered that once he had decided to quit his job with the Agriculture Ministry, it took years for them to accept his resignation. Senior officers employed by the government of India must follow a protocol to resign. Viney had ignored that process by leaving the country without permission. As a result, he was technically still employed by the ministry and could go back to his job. Whether in practice he could go back and just pick up where he left off was something we never needed to find out.

The position in Iraq itself was quite interesting and fulfilling. The company employed about 2,000 TCNs, hailing from Pakistan, the Philippines, Thailand, and many Arab countries like Tunisia and Egypt. Viney was the odd man out, being the only employee from India. The office environment was multicultural and provided a great learning experience to deal with a total of twenty nationalities as Human Resources Director. From interest and a desire to be respectful, Viney learned some words in the various languages and inquired about the cultures of everyone with whom he worked. The company provided Viney with a car for business and personal use. Since construction was taking place a ways from the office and city, this was a necessity. However, he was one of the few third country nationals (TCNs) granted this privilege. Coupled with the fact that Viney administered personnel policies for TCNs, who were treated separately from employees from Western countries, it was difficult not to think of TCN as a derogatory designation arousing a feeling of inferiority when compared to European and North American colleagues.

That feeling was both ameliorated and reinforced when Viney convinced the company to let his family join him in April 1982. On the one hand, we were delighted that we were granted something normally reserved only for Westerners. On the other hand, we had a twinge of guilt that we were an exception to the rules. Regardless, we were ecstatic to be reunited. Megha, our daughter, was still a toddler. After not seeing her father for five months (about one-quarter of her lifetime!), she didn't recognize her father at first glance. It was painful.

Today, we see commercials in which young parents separated from their children have video calls home. While that certainly would have been a welcome technology for us in 1982, it may have been useless anyway. Due to the war and Iraq's underdeveloped infrastructure, telecommunications were hard to find and unreliable even when we could use a telephone. The positive result of us being separated was the opportunity to become reacquainted while learning about our new home. Viney had learned a few things about life in Iraq, but there was still much to figure out to feel at ease.

Saddam Hussein had his portraits almost everywhere there was space to place one. When Kumud arrived in Iraq for the first time, she noticed a large billboard near the airport carrying his image. She asked if this was the portrait of a movie star, given that billboards in India often displayed film celebrities. After explaining, Viney had to caution Kumud not to speak anything negative about Saddam Hussein at any time. Even spouses would not speak anything bad about Iraq's leader in case their own spouse was an informer. Just this aspect alone of living in Iraq gave us a new appreciation for the freedoms of speech, press, and expression we enjoyed in India. However, we did recognize that the limitations in Iraq did not arise from the culture, but just from what the rulers felt was a political necessity.

Iraq is a secular Muslim country, meaning Islamic precepts are a matter of personal choice, rather than legal strictures. Women were free to work and drive. They were not required to wear the traditional *burqa* that covers the entire body except the eyes and feet. Woman would cover their heads with scarves, but men also frequently covered their heads, especially in rural areas. One wonders how Muslims in different countries interpret the Quran so differently that some places are quite relaxed and liberal, and others, as we discovered later in Saudi Arabia, impose restrictions they insist are requirements of Allah found in the Quran.

Kumud, unfortunately, was not able to take advantage of women being allowed to work. An expat's visa entitles him to work but prohibits his spouse from working unless she has her own visa permitting work. Kumud gave up her bank job to join Viney, even though she had great credentials. Luckily, it was not necessary for us to have two incomes. Also, not working freed Kumud to look after Megha, a clear benefit since our families were not there to help, and to become comfortable in this new environment.

We initially lived in Shomeli, a village near Babylon (150 kilometers from Baghdad), for the rest of 1982. We rented a house that had been given to a war widow. Soldiers killed in the Iran-Iraq War were considered martyrs, so their widows were given special considerations. This woman chose to remain in her existing home and make some money renting the house provided to her as a martyr's widow. The building was newly constructed, but the work was so shoddy that the walls were falling in by the time we moved out. Of course, with shortages of everything due to war, we doubt anything much better could have been provided, and it was in some ways an improvement over the place she chose to use for herself.

Everyone was very generous, ensuring we felt welcome. Neighbors in the village sent over food and such. Villagers nearby also invited us to lunch now and then. One time, we were asked if we could eat fowl. We said that yes, we could. Someone brought a chicken into the room where Viney was with the other men while the women sat together in a front room. The chicken was killed right in front of Viney. As anyone unused to such a thing, the scene was very difficult to watch, and disturbing. After the chicken had been cooked, we ate the flesh with the blood stains still on the floor. The whole experience was peculiar. The month of Ramadan, during which Muslims fast from dawn to dusk every day, provided a more pleasant experience. Every day for 30 days, we received delicacies from neighbors specially prepared for Ramadan for the evening meal breaking the fast.

During 1981-83, Viney's brother Krishan was teaching engineering to Iraqi Army officers. He and his family lived in Baghdad. Heading down to see them every two weeks was a pleasant diversion from the village life in Shomeli. Those visits exposed us to the modern city life in Baghdad, a capital on par with any other city in those days. Given its size and prominence, the city had much better shopping than anywhere else in Iraq. Also, since telecommunications were so rudimentary in the country, it was nearly impossible to call our relatives in India from anywhere except Baghdad during that first year.

In 1983, we moved to the company's French Camp, where European and North American employees lived in more than 200 villas. Although it was called a camp, the housing consisted of portable villas that could be moved as needed to another location. We stayed there until 1985. That was a unique experience to be able to witness and understand French and Western culture for the first time. The emphasis was definitely on providing creature comforts for the European and North American employees and their families. The store was stocked with imported food of all kinds. For recreation, the camp offered a swimming pool, tennis courts, and billiard tables. Needless to say, living there was a huge difference compared to a small Iraqi village. In fact, the camp was quite different from anywhere we had lived in India, too. In many ways, it was almost a small European town.

The European feel was reinforced by the exclusiveness of who lived there. Aside from two high-ranking Pakistani employees, we were the only TCNs in the French Camp and the only ones who were allowed to have our families with us. In this environment, we experienced a big paradigm shift. We realized rather quickly that the former colonial masters were no different than we, that brown people are the same as white people. Perhaps this concept may be difficult for readers to grasp if they do not come from or have never lived in a place where colonialism is a recent and omnipresent part of history. While Americans and Canadians still have problems involving prejudice based on skin color, they have not had the added burden of one group governing another for many decades. When we were in Iraq, it had been only 35 years since Britain left India and just 20 years or so after Britain, France, and other European countries granted independence to most of their colonies.

Since the compound was operated for Western employees of a French company, many of the residents were from France. We made many friendships with our French neighbors. One family even sent their sixteen-year-old son to live with us as an exchange student in the U.S. in 1995. A French lady friend taught Kumud how to swim. Viney also learned to swim while there. We also studied the basics of French and Arabic. It was a blessing to enjoy simple conversations with Iraqis and French in their native languages. This impressed upon us how easy it is to demonstrate one's interest in the people you meet through simple gestures such as this. We could not have had this opportunity in India.

Summer temperatures in Iraq average 100 degrees Fahrenheit during the day and 80 degrees Fahrenheit at night. During the cooler winter months, daytime temperatures hover around 60 degrees Fahrenheit. There is no particular rainy season in Iraq. The summer months do not see much rain at all. Most of the rainfall comes during December and January. The average yearly rainfall totals below 10 inches. As one would expect given these very dry conditions, Iraq is mostly beige-yellow dust and grayish rocks. Except in the fields, there is little vegetation. Being so close to ancient Babylon, we could only wonder at the creativity of the people who built irrigation works to support any sizable population in this area known as the Cradle of Civilization.

Two of the great pleasures of living overseas or even visiting a place for an extended period is that one can go beneath the surface of a culture and see much more than just the usual tourist sites. Back then, Iraq was quite open to exploration by foreigners. In fact, the government made some efforts to promote both casual and academic visitors to experience the many ancient landmarks spread primarily along the Tigris and Euphrates Rivers that gave the area its old name in Greek: Mesopotamia, the land between rivers. While living in Iraq, we took a road trip to Mosul, Erbil, and Kirkuk in the north. Two other families joined us as we traveled in a large van, just three couples and four kids.

The northern area is mainly Kurdish territory, although currently it is mostly under the control of the Islamic State. After World War I, the Kurds tried to have a homeland called Kurdistan recognized at the Versailles Peace Conference. Instead, they wound up distributed among Turkey, Syria, Iraq, and Iran. Kurds are very open and friendly with customs more similar to Turks than Arabs. Mosul lies quite far from Baghdad, just under 250 miles north-northeast of the capital.

The second largest city in Iraq at the time, Mosul had a mixed Christian and Muslim population, with the two faiths living very harmoniously. Some Christians lived in Baghdad, but the community was not as noticeable. The Christians throughout Iraq have mostly fled in the wake of sectarian violence after the U.S.-led invasion and the rise of the Islamic State. Tolerance of religions other than Islam was pervasive in Iraq. For example, shops do not close during Islamic prayer times as they do in Saudi Arabia and other less secular countries. We found it very interesting to visit a church in a region that was one of the earliest areas where Christianity was established.

The food in Mosul was absolutely delicious. Coffee was ubiquitous and excellent, just as it is throughout the Middle East. The drive from Mosul to Erbil is particularly scenic, with many hills. Erbil contained several very old churches, including one that had been listed as one of the prestigious UNESCO World Heritage Sites. We find it surprising that the Iraqi government has pretty much abandoned Mosul and most of the north to the Islamic State. It indicates an unfortunate decision to abandon the harmony that once existed and allow extremists to impose severely harsh intolerance on a once peaceful and enchanting region.

On our way back to Baghdad, we stopped in Tikrit to eat. Tikrit is Saddam Hussein's birthplace. Reminders throughout the town made it clear this was a special place. Actually, though, there was nothing much special there. In a country full of monuments created by numerous civilizations stretching back five thousand years, Tikrit is just a small town with no remarkable features. Unlike Mosul, the Iraqi government retook Tikrit from the Islamic State in March 2015.

We also availed ourselves of an opportunity to visit Karbala and Najaf, two holy cities for Shi'ites. Najaf holds the tomb of Alī ibn Abī Tālib or Imām Alī, the First Imam of the Shiites. He was a cousin and son-in-law of the Prophet Mohammed. While Sunnis consider him to be a legitimate caliph (leader of the Islamic community), the Shi'a consider him to be the righteous caliph. Shi'ites view the golden-domed Imam Ali Mosque as the third most holy site (along with the Imam Hussain Shrine in Karbala), after Makkah and Medina in Saudi Arabia. As such, the mosque receives the third most pilgrims of any site holy to Muslims. To Sunnis, Jerusalem ranks third due to its prominence in the story of Abraham being asked to sacrifice his son and as the location where the Prophet ascended to heaven in The Night Journey. Kumud entered the mosque but was wearing an abayah (black robe covering all but the head, hands, and feet), so no one may have known she was not Muslim. Such a thing could never happen in Makkah. Non-Muslims are not allowed anywhere near the holy places in Saudi Arabia and are forbidden from entering mosques.

Karbala is famed for the Imam Hussein Shrine, which houses the tomb of Al-Hussein ibn Ali. He was the son of Imam Ali and Fatimah, the daughter of Mohammed. As with his father's tomb, Hussein's burial place is a pilgrimage site for Shi'a Muslims. Many pilgrims walk the 80 kilometers from Najaf to Karbala to be there on the anniversary of the Battle of Karbala. In 680 CE, Hussein and his brother Abbas died challenging the authority of the Umayyad caliph. Their revolt established the split between Shi'a and Sunni Muslims. Crowds all day long visit the shrine, just as Muslims do on hajj to Makkah. More than 35 million pilgrims per year visit the shrine. Although Sunnis ruled under Saddam Hussein, the Shi'a community was given leeway to govern these holy places. Since Najaf and Karbala are far south of Baghdad, they have not been overrun by the Islamic State, which enforces ruthlessly strict Sunni principles. In fact, the Shi'a-led government today would take extra precautions to avoid that happening.

By far the best event of our years in Iraq was the birth of our son. We made a decision to have our son's delivery in Iraq. We also decided that we were going to surprise our families in India. We didn't tell them Kumud was pregnant and didn't even tell them she had delivered our second child until we returned to India two months after he was born. We took a chance that they would be offended by our silence, but we knew everyone would be most pleased and happy for us and would forgive us for keeping her pregnancy secret.

Staying in Iraq for this pregnancy was a gamble. The delivery was to take place in an Iraqi hospital in Diwaniya, the nearest town, which is 30 miles away. The French doctor in the Camp saw Kumud each week. For the last month of her pregnancy, a company ambulance was at our call right at our residence. When the time came at 1:00 am on September 19, 1984, we were shocked upon getting to the hospital; it was not anything like the doctor had said. The hospital did not have much equipment or extensive facilities. Although it was as large as the hospitals in India, the services were very basic. Then the midwives could not handle the delivery, and we waited for the doctor, who arrived in the morning. However, the timing didn't seem to matter too much when we discovered that they discharged mothers within a few hours of delivery.

Our son was born at 10:20 a.m. The nurse rushed out of the delivery room with a big smile on her face as she said, "Mubarak, huwa walad," meaning, "Congratulations, it is a boy." The words were music to Viney's ears. She was rewarded with all the cash he had at hand. At 3:30 p.m., just over five hours after delivery, Kumud was discharged. While she was being discharged, we were asked what name we wanted to give our baby son.

Bearing in mind that in 1984 the leader of Iraq was respected for standing up to the clerics ruling Iran, our readers may be less inclined to wonder why we named our newborn son Saddam Kaushal. As we mentioned, Saddam Hussein had his portraits in every nook and corner of Iraq. He was feared as an authoritarian dictator whose legitimacy was grounded on his ability to keep the disparate populations in Iraq at peace with one another through the Ba'ath Party and the war with Iran. It was not unusual then, or even now, for Western democracies to ally themselves with dictators just so long as they were the "right" kind, meaning willing to support Western interests.

One can live under an authoritarian regime and remain largely ignorant of its worst practices, but when one's life intersects with those practices, there can no longer be any question that the citizens pay a terrifying price for the stability dictators usually bring. Viney saw firsthand how alleged lawbreakers were treated by the regime. A TCN working for the company was arrested and sent to Abu Ghraib prison. Viney had to meet the employee in this infamous prison 20 miles outside Baghdad. His difficult task was to comfort the employee that efforts were being made to have him released and deported. While Abu Ghraib has since become associated with the interrogation tactics performed by Americans against captured members of Hussein's government, at that time it was as notorious in Iraq as Guantanamo, the Bastille, or the Peter and Paul Fortress have been as a hell hole reserved as much for political prisoners as for actual criminals. But most of the world either did not know or did not care. It wasn't until 1990 when he ordered the invasion of Kuwait that everyone united in deciding that Saddam Hussein was evil. Our Iraq stay made us learn many lessons.

- *Suffering is never right.* The Iraqi people were very pleasant, but they were extremely fearful of the political establishment as represented by Saddam Hussein's Ba'ath Party. We found ill feelings about the regime among many of the Iraqis we met, but they would not say anything openly. Before we could finish asking a question, they would put a finger to their lips to indicate we should be silent. The younger generation was sacrificed in a war that left more than 500,000 soldiers and 500,000 civilians dead on both sides. It was sad that the country's leadership let this happen, misjudging the tenacity of the Iranian regime and ignoring its own stubbornness. The war was useless, which made Iraqis grow increasingly concerned about their own regime. Iraqis should not have had to go through that very long war, suffering years of deprivation made worse by their country's lack of development to begin with. Kumud was reminded of all of the places we had known when watching the U.S.-led invasion in 2002-03.

- *Some countries need some degree of authoritarian rule.* Iraq is a made-up country whose borders were created after World War I by Europeans who thought Arabs were Arabs and who ignored the request of the Kurdish people to have their own country. Although Saddam's rule was authoritarian, he still acted as a glue to keep the country united. Iraq's Muslim population was 60 percent Shi'a and 40 percent Sunni. The different factions lived peacefully, though very distrustful of each other. Even the minority Christians felt safe. The Shi'ites resented that they were excluded from government but could not express their frustration in any disruptive fashion. In many ways, Iraq was better off than it has been since 2002, even though order was enforced by threats and oppression. Although suffering is never right, one must recognize that stability usually creates less overall pain than chaos.

- *Your roots inspire you to excel.* Wherever one resides, your motherland always remains a part of you, and one part of you always remains in your motherland. Being the only Indian in a company with more than two thousand employees, Viney had a moral obligation to prove their trust in hiring him for a leadership position. He did not disappoint them and did an exceptional job. He was the first TCN to get permission for his wife to join him, and Kumud arrived in Iraq with our daughter within three months of Viney joining the company.

Kumud and Varun, 1987 in Cyprus
(before we entered
Turkey side by oversight)

Sandrine de Kerhuel – Iraq 1983
In a traditional Indian Saree
(Kumud's hobby was to dress
all French women in
Indian Sarees)

Kumud, Megha, and Varun in Iraq
1989 (Saddam Hussein's guests)

Viney, Iraq - 1985
A typical Kurdish dress

Kaushal Family in Iraq 1989 with the
Then Information Minister of Iraq
We were Saddam Hussein's guests

First Interlude:
England and France (1983-84)

"One of the great things about travel is
that you find out how many good, kind people there are."
Edith Wharton

During our Iraq stay, we had a chance to visit England and France during December 1983 to January 1984. It was our first exposure to Europe other than what we had gleaned from reading and our time in the French Camp. This month-long trip opened our eyes to a different world. Indeed, our time in these two countries inspired us to emigrate. We appreciated the favorable living conditions and the absence of scarcity. At the time, the idea was to move to Europe. However, the seed planted on this trip ended up laying the foundation for our eventual immigration to Canada.

England was our first exposure to a Western country. It was an eye-opener, particularly coming from war-torn Iraq. The shops were flooded with items of all sorts. Scarcity such as we had encountered in Iraq was completely absent. Our visit coincided with preparations for Christmas and the holiday itself. Large cities all over the world that celebrate Christmas are even more active than at other times of the year, and definitely more festive. We were most impressed with the markdowns and sales, particularly after Christmas Day.

We stayed with Kumud's younger sister and her family in their home in the Southall area of west London. Southall supported a thriving Punjabi community and still does. In fact, Southall now has a majority of residents from India or Pakistan. The markets had a Punjabi touch, and one could find everything that would be available in Punjab. The markets were not the only reminder of home. It seemed people lived like they lived back home. They engaged in similar social gatherings, the talk centered on wealth and money (although the money was the British pound, rather than the Indian rupee), and the familiar Indian festivals remained on the calendar of major events. We even had the opportunity to visit a Sikh *gurdwara* (temple) and Hare Rama Hare Krishna temple.

India has some huge cities, but we had spent our lives in secondary cities and places like Shillong that are quite modest in size. London is vast. Westminster, the various palaces, the great roundabouts (circuses from the same root word as circle) and squares, the bridges crossing the Thames, the parks and memorials, and the world-class museums all add up overwhelmingly. Further afield are Windsor Castle and its Great Park. The metropolis has been inspiring awe among first-time visitors for centuries, even English people from the Midlands, North, and West Country. Fortunately, London has a well-developed transportation system. Double-decker buses and large, black taxicabs are icons. The Underground or Tube (subway) was very impressive to us, having never seen this form of transportation before. Fortunately, Kumud's brother-in-law took off time from work to shepherd us around.

Some of the highlights of our visit were finding new experiences, both fun and provocative. We recall having front row seats at an aquarium with a dolphin show. We were soaking wet right after the dolphin made its first jump. We went to Speaker's Corner in Hyde Park, an area set aside for open-air public speaking, debate, and discussion. We were intrigued that ordinary people could voice their opinions on any subject openly. While this would not be unusual in India, it was a sea change from Iraq, where media reports and freedom of speech were strictly curtailed. Even the simplest things caught our attention. Before our visit to London, we had never seen or heard of public launderettes (or laundromats) with washers and dryers. We were a bit shocked to see people taking dirty laundry to be washed in the open like that. After all, to air one's dirty laundry means to let the world know the worst about your family.

A big paradigm shift for us was the interactions we saw between Indians and English people. The Britishers ruled over India for centuries. We considered them and were taught to consider them superior to Asians in every respect. Kumud's sister and husband had a British couple as tenants. As landlords, they had put restrictions on the couple regarding how much cooking they did, how often they could shower, and how loud they could play music. Wow! Indians could restrict Britishers in their own country!

Despite this revelation, reminders of colonialism are everywhere one turns in London. For us, the most somber moment came when we visited the Tower of London. We were not moved so much by the reminders of so many people executed or imprisoned there. The Crown Jewels are stored there. One of the most important objects in the collection is the Koh-I-Noor diamond, a gem confiscated by Lord Dalhousie as a "spoil of war" when the British East India Company signed an unequal treaty with the Maharajah of Lahore, ending the Sikh War. The diamond was given to Queen Victoria in 1850, whose husband ordered it cut by almost a third and made into a brooch for his wife. After Victoria's death, it became the centerpiece in the crown worn by the female consort of a male British monarch.

Viewing this piece of history that had been revered as the eye in the statue of a Hindu goddess before becoming a prize fought over by Mughal emperors, Persian invaders, and local kings in Punjab, we could not help but mourn that something so valuable to India, not in monetary terms but cultural, should remain in London. India has formally asked for the return of the Koh-I-Noor but has been rebuffed by the current British Prime Minister, who claims returning the diamond would be "illogical."

The New Year celebrations were amazing. Even more amazing was the sight of ladies and gentlemen alike going around kissing and hugging. Viney was shocked to have a policewoman come up to him and hug him. Such openness between the sexes, even at a party, was a big shift from what we had been experiencing in Iraq or knew from India.

We took the ferry from Dover to France during the first week of January. It was interesting to see personal cars of people being loaded on the ship. It never crossed our minds that people would do that. Then again, who would have thought it was possible to build the Channel Tunnel so cars and trains can cross without needing a ship?

Our experience was the French do not want to speak English, even if they know the language well. Perhaps it is the lasting memory of French replacing Latin as the language of diplomacy and *lingua franca* throughout Europe. Perhaps people are not very friendly with English-speaking foreigners due to the historical rivalry between the British and the French. For us, the French refusal to acknowledge English was a blessing. We had to learn basic day-to-day French to get even the simplest things done. My boss in Iraq with the French company arranged to lend us his vacant condo in Paris for a week. It was in the heart of the city. We loved the place. The Metro, Paris' subway system, is known for its unique Art Deco designed station signs. It should be equally famed for being easy to navigate. Of course, having learned from using the Tube in London, we were familiar with the basics. French food is as well-known in the world as very special and refined with many courses. Indeed, English has adopted a fair number of the course names, such as hors d'oeurves, entrée, and dessert.

We spent the week visiting most of the historical places in the city: Notre Dame Cathedral; Champs Elysees; Musée du Louvre; Eiffel Tower; Arc de Triomphe; Moulin Rouge Night Cabaret; and many others. Like most tourists, we also traveled to see the Chateau de Versailles, the grand palace and gardens built by the Sun King, Louis XIV. So much has been written about these sites, there is nothing for us to add. This trip did reinforce the importance of going out in the world to see the buildings, streets, monuments, and museums that one has become familiar with through books, movies, or pictures. Nothing can substitute for the feeling one has later of seeing a picture of the Eiffel Tower and thinking, "I have been there!"

During a later trip to Paris in 1993, we had a chance to stay in Paris with one of Viney's French bosses from our days in Iraq. Paris was experiencing a water shortage. Taking a shower was not common. Instead, one had to take a bath at specific hours with limited water. We know droughts occur in the U.S., and California has been particularly hurt by a lack of rain in recent years. However, water has always been scarce in the Western states given that the region is mostly one large desert. Who would think northern France would experience a water shortage? We also noticed that Parisian apartments are very small compared to those in the U.S. In less than ten years, we had experienced enough to compare Europe to North America, just as we earlier compared Europe to India and Iraq. Before, we were impressed with how advanced Europe was and how much easier life was. On our second visit, we saw that advancement and ease are relative.

Spending this time in a materially more advanced part of the world gave us just as different a perspective as having moved around in India or living in Iraq. Aside from the memories and goods we took back with us, we also learned fresh insights.

- *History permeates a place and influences the present more than most people realize.* Everywhere one looks in London and Paris, buildings and monuments remind residents and visitors alike of the past. Even though France and Great Britain have been allies since the Crimean War, animosity and barriers remained apparent on our visit. While 1853 to 1984 may seem like a long time that span pales in comparison to eight centuries of rivalry and war. Even as allies, they competed for colonies, trade, and primacy. Today, Trafalgar Square and the Arc de Triomphe herald victories against the other nation.
- *Language is critical to absorb any culture.* This is not just a matter of the French thinking they should not have to speak English. Even a few simple sentences and words spoken in the local tongue make people open up. Also, all languages have words and phrases that cannot be properly translated. To get the true feeling for a place, one must make some effort to understand it from the viewpoint of the residents. That requires knowing at least some of their language.
- *Complaining about the weather is universal.* We were fed up with so much sunshine in the Middle East and were shocked by the cold temperatures in Shillong. Then again, even in Punjab one begins to get a bit tired of the weather at some point in the rainy season. The people in England and France were dying to enjoy sunny days. They would have been thrilled to spend some time in cloudless Iraq. On the other hand, they are used to cold weather every winter and prepared for it. Most likely, they would know enough to pack a few sweaters if they were traveling to India's northeast.
- *The simplest things can be markedly different.* Currency is the most obvious item that differs from country to country. Even nowadays with the euro, each country designs its own coins and bills, but at least the conversion rate is the same everywhere it is

used. Other differences are more relics of national pride than simple preferences. In England they drive on the left side, while in France they drive on the right. The English still use the Imperial system of miles, yards, feet, and inches to measure distances and pounds and ounces for weights, while the French have stuck with the Revolution's metric system of kilometers, meters, centimeters, kilograms and grams. The English even throw in oddities like a stone, which equals 14 pounds, to indicate body weight.

Second Interlude:
Kuwait and Turkey (1981, 1984, and 1985)

"The journey, not the arrival, matters."
T. S. Eliot

Viney recounts:

When I first went to Iraq in mid-December 1981, I had to fly via Kuwait. Due to the Iraq-Iran War, no commercial airlines could fly to Baghdad directly except Iraqi Airways. I took a Kuwait Airways flight from Delhi to Kuwait and then traveled by road to Baghdad, a distance of 430 miles.

This was the first time I had left India. I was nervous to be in a Muslim country because I did not want to break any laws, but I was unfamiliar with what the laws might be. I met some expats at the airport, as well as in the city. From our conversations, I thought they seemed happy with the international schools and health care provided. I wasn't prepared to see international restaurants and fast food chains. It was interesting to see a prosperous Arab country at that time.

The drive took more than 10 hours. While going by road from Kuwait to Iraq, I could see large junkyards with all brands of cars dumped in them. In India, we were used to seeing only a couple of brands and no foreign makes. Here so many shiny, good looking cars were just dumped. Years later in 1982, my brother drove from Baghdad to Kuwait to buy a car and picked up a good Toyota for $400. I learned cars were dirt cheap in Kuwait. When my brother left Iraq in 1983, he gave that car to me. I used it for a couple of years in Iraq before giving it to a Pakistani family who took it to Islamabad.

My 1984 visit just reconfirmed my observations of 1981. Kuwait was, like many Gulf countries, rich from oil. The government used those riches to bring in cheap labor and pricier exports rather than develop the skills of its citizens. Instead, residents enjoyed the benefits of government largesse.

Kuwait is one of several countries in the world where the indigenous population is small and government revenues from petroleum are substantial. Kuwait has chosen to spread the wealth among its citizens. While this sounds quite nice, it is also quite risky.

- *Abundance spoils people.* The revenue that nature provides and prosperity that the country enjoys are precarious. Income earned through hard work may seem onerous to people, but they also gain satisfaction from being productive and being rewarded for being productive. Kuwait did not develop local talent and was highly dependent on foreign workers, practices that are not sustainable in the long run.
- *Dependence does not make people rich.* Kuwait exists because the local ruling family was able to monopolize petroleum extraction. The ruling family is dependent on oil revenues, and Kuwaitis are dependent on the distribution of a portion of those oil revenues. In essence, Kuwaitis are paid to be Kuwaiti. Saddam Hussein saw this cycle of dependence. He decided to end it and acquire the oil revenues to benefit him and Iraq. So he invaded Kuwait in 1990. The world's response shocked him. Although the Iraqi occupation was brief, the Gulf War ruined much of Kuwait. Kuwaiti citizens, who had never been expected to be productive, now had no means of support and no way to obtain income until the oil revenues started again.

We also visited Turkey in 1985 along with a French couple, Mr. and Mrs. Daniel Lente. Megha, our four-year-old daughter, was a friend of Nicolas, their son. Our son, Varun, was just eight months old. The Lentes had French passports and did not need a visa to go to Turkey. They breezed right through immigration in Istanbul. We had Indian passports and landed without a visa in Turkey because we were under the impression that a visa was not needed. We did need visas. The immigration officer said we should have gotten visas in Baghdad. We explained that we didn't realize this and were traveling with a French couple that had just cleared passport control. The officer went to his superior. When his superior saw that we were accompanied by two small children, he was sympathetic. Being with a French family helped us as well. Additionally, we had explained that Viney had a good job waiting in Iraq, so we weren't going to stay in Turkey except for our planned vacation. This was well before 9/11, which made entering countries much stricter. Under the circumstances, they gave us visas on arrival as an exception.

During the flight was one of the first times we saw women changing clothes on an airplane, a routine we would become familiar with. One by one, women in burqas got up to use the toilet and came out sans burqa. Most were dressed quite nicely in Western fashions. It was most interesting that so many of the women were so beautiful as a result of never being in the sun at home. Overall, this experience demonstrated that people will grab any freedom available whenever they can. Indeed, at the time Turkey was a liberal society. Although Turkey is a Muslim country, the government established in the 1920s after the fall of the Ottoman Empire sought to make the country more Western, secular, and open. Men and women mingle freely and share doing all chores. Women even ran shops. The interpretation of Islam regarding women was very different than anywhere in the Middle East.

We rented a car with the Lentes, which gave us great mobility within Turkey. Primarily, we stayed in Istanbul. However, we also drove along the coast into the countryside for a couple of days. Our French companions wanted fresh seafood almost every day, since that was uncommon in the interior of Iraq.

We distinctly remember we were moving through a souk (market) in Istanbul to buy carpets. One of the shopkeepers stopped us and asked us if we were Hindi. He meant whether we were from India/Hindustan. We responded in the affirmative. He started giving us his condolences for the big tragedy that had happened earlier that June day. We thought there must have been riots or a natural disaster at home. Actually, an Air India plane on a Montreal-London-Delhi flight was destroyed by a bomb by Babbar Khalsa, a Sikh militant organization. All 329 passengers and crew died. Most of the victims were Indian-Canadians. The bombing remains the deadliest attack on a single airplane. At the time, events like this were very unusual. It was a very sad moment for us. Many shopkeepers expressed their condolences to us.

We really must stop to explain just how significant it was to us that the tragedy occurred and that foreigners demonstrated their sympathy. The Turks we encountered that day grieved for the dead from the plane explosion. What we knew and they most likely did not was the background, the tragedies that had occurred before the airplane bombing. Babbar Khalsa was seeking revenge for Operation Blue Star. Sikhs wanted a separate homeland and had fortified the Harmandir Sahib Complex (aka the Golden Temple), the Vatican of Sikhs in Amritsar, Punjab. Prime Minister Indira Gandhi ordered the Indian Army to take control of the place. Part of the operation included rounding up Sikhs who wore kirpans, a ceremonial knife, and had weapons and were protesting the attack on Harmandir Sahib. Officially, almost 500 civilians and 156 soldiers died as a result of the operation. However, given the artillery shelling in crowded Amritsar, some sources have claimed that thousands of civilians were killed. Sikhs in the Army mutinied all across the country. Many Sikhs resigned from the Army and returned honors they had received from the Indian Government. Then in October 1984, Indira Gandhi was assassinated by two of her Sikh bodyguards. Other Indians, particularly members of the Congress Party, were outraged. Anti-Sikh riots left more than 3,000 Sikhs dead. The entire episode demonstrated how fragile the balance can be in a country that contains so many different religious and ethnic communities. The concern we encountered in the Turkish market probably had nothing to do with why the plane was bombed. It was just an expression of human compassion to strangers.

Genuine compassion is invaluable. In a way, it was ironic to find it in a marketplace. Our visit to the souk on that tragic day was one of many shopping trips. It is critical to seriously conduct negotiations in Turkish markets. Many Western tourists are not used to negotiating for purchases and thus end up paying very high prices for goods. One should get at least 50 percent off the first price the vendor asks for. We were better prepared since the same type of negotiations take place in India. We bought a few small carpets for only 25 percent of the asking price. Turkish hand-made carpets are considered to be among the finest in the world. They are comparable to Iranian (Persian) carpets. The yarn is pure wool. A family of three can spend six months making a rug. While Westerners might not get the best deal possible in the souk, the rugs are still much less expensive than in the U.S. or Europe.

In addition to negotiating, one also must be careful about what items are bought. A supposedly hand-woven carpet could have been made by machine. Bronze plates or coffee sets, which have intricate designs, may not be bronze or may be so shabbily made they become dented easily. Most importantly, visitors cannot remove antiques of any kind. Customs checks departing passengers' bags very thoroughly.

It was interesting to interact with Turkish people. The customary Arabic greeting, *as-salaam 'alaykum*, was understood, but we also learned *merhaba,* which means "Hi!" in Turkish. Almost everywhere, we were offered coffee. Turkish coffee is very special and a big draw for all. Shops selling Turkish coffee are everywhere. Another common sight is Turkish men smoking using a hookah. Even during meals, they smoke at intervals between eating. Speaking of eating, one of our favorite dishes was mussels stuffed with aromatic rice called *midye dolmas*. Clearly, the Turks find them irresistible. They are widely available, even at roadside stands.

We were pleasantly surprised at how warm and friendly Turks are to Indians. We discovered that Turkish families love Indian Bollywood movies. People know all of the leading actors by name and film, especially Amitabh Bachchan. We were welcomed in every shop by salesmen proudly reciting the names of the Indian movies they had seen. They also listed their favorite songs. Beyond movies, we found Turks were familiar with India generally. Their knowledge resulted from the long history of contact with Muslims from India since colonial times, when Pakistan was part of British India.

Many of the lessons we learned from our visit to Turkey were things we had experienced before but appreciated being reminded of.

- *Go native to the extent possible.* Travel provides a wonderful opportunity to taste local foods and expand your palate. Eating food from a Turkish restaurant in Chicago is nothing like the experience of having the foods prepared in their country of origin. We never would have encountered a treat as delicious as a *midye dolma* had we not been to Turkey.

- *Negotiate.* Whether one has any experience bargaining with a shopkeeper or not, it is always worthwhile to try to get the lowest price possible. If your initial bid is shockingly low, you won't be kicked out (usually), no matter how appalled the vendor responds. The owner of a market stall still wants to make a sale. Consider it a game that you very much would like to win. Believe us, the shopkeeper will still be making a profit, or she won't accept your final offer. And it has nothing to do with how much money you have versus how poor the vendor is. If you want to be charitable or feel guilty about how much you paid, give bigger tips to people who help you or find a religious institution or other place that helps the needy. The market stall owner will have better luck with the next American who comes along and doesn't bargain.
- *Societies in which women have greater freedom are much more interesting than those that don't.* In Turkey, the sexes are treated almost equally. We know that except in the rare matriarchal societies like the ones we experienced in Shillong, women struggle to be accepted as just as talented, able, and valuable as men. Given the legal rights needed to demonstrate these qualities, women will use them to prove they are only different, but still equal, to men. Being able to enjoy how women participate differently provides a much richer environment for residents and visitors alike. This became incredibly clear to us during the next stage of our odyssey.

Saudi Arabia (1985-1990)

"You have two qualities which God, the Most Exalted,
likes and loves.
One is mildness, and the other is toleration."
Prophet Muhammad: Riyadh us-Saleheen Volume 1:632

After four years in Iraq, we moved to Riyadh, the capital city of the Kingdom of Saudi Arabia, at the behest of the French company Viney worked for. Our time in Saudi Arabia from October 1985 to February 1990 will always stay a bittersweet chapter of our lives. Would we go back? Probably not. We have several stories to tell that will explain the "not" part of that answer. In fact, the bulk of this chapter contains our recollections of incidents that justify avoiding any visits to the Kingdom. But there are valid, rational grounds for qualifying "not" with "probably."

All countries are unique. Saudi Arabia stands out. The country moves forward rapidly in terms of infrastructure and services while simultaneously it stands inertly on political and social issues. Construction in Riyadh has continued since our stay to the present, with modern structures and huge malls as fancy as the best in the U.S. In the late 1980s, it was a great city to live in because it was exciting to see the expansion and development. The same remains true today. On the other hand, one must get used to the prayer times, when everything closes down. Hearing the call to prayer in the morning on speakers coming from mosques all over the city indicates a new day has started, not just for you, but for the entire community.

From a purely practical, economic point of view, the Kingdom is a great place to be employed for a few years. The cost of living was and remains quite affordable. Food, cleaning products, and other needed goods are widely available and priced reasonably. Even gold with high karat value is everywhere, for great prices. Many foreigners, especially Westerners, are given housing and an automobile as part of their compensation. Even if this is not the case, rents are relatively well-priced. It would not be unusual to save at least sixty percent of one's salary after paying expenses. This makes it a desirable place to work for people from all over the world. In three or four years, one can save enough to have a down payment for a $500,000 home. The laws can sound scary, and following the dress code can be difficult, but putting up with some inconveniences and anxiety certainly are worth the benefit of spending so little of one's salary.

People in Saudi Arabia can be quite charming and gracious, particularly if they are used to being around expats or have traveled. Our neighbor next door was also our landlord. He had studied in the United States and lived there with his wife for a couple of years. We would categorize him as mildly Westernized. His wife invited us to her home. Kumud was led to the women's wing by a maid, while Viney went to the men's wing. The maid would come back when Viney was in the foyer, waiting to meet her to go.

Soon, our landlord's wife asked Kumud to meet without husbands at our house. She brought friends, and they talked about husbands and children, as well as Arabic and Saudi culture. They visited every so often. Kumud would make Indian snacks that they loved due to the spices. Unlike many Saudi women, who can be quite shy, our neighbor's wife was open to meeting foreigners having lived in the U.S. We developed such a good relationship that our landlord said he was eventually going to have to pay us to stay. Indeed, the villa in which we lived was very nice, but it was a golden jail for Kumud.

Women bear the brunt of the social restrictions arising from the Saudi adoption of a very conservative form of Islam called Wahhabism. As with other religions, different schools of thought arise over the centuries as to how to interpret God's will. There are several varieties of Judaism, even though the number of believers is comparatively small. Christianity is well known for its many schisms dating back to the first century and the wide range of denominations that have resulted. As we mentioned about Iraq's population split, Islam is primarily divided between Shi'a and Sunni, each claiming to follow the true line of leaders following the Prophet Mohammed. But even within these two groups, there are many subdivisions. The most important for non-Muslims is whether the government of a predominantly Muslim country chooses to be secular and avoids basing laws on Islamic law (*sharia*) or formulates laws primarily or strictly from *sharia*. Saudi Arabia, which is home to the holiest places in Islam, falls into the latter category. As a result, women are treated in a fashion that seems quite dated and demeaning.

Most famously, women are not allowed to drive in the Kingdom. They can have a company driver take them to the market for groceries. Women in more well-to-do families may have a chauffeur. However, most of the time women must be accompanied by one of her closest male relatives, like a husband, father, or brother. Whoever is driving with a woman in the vehicle must always have papers demonstrating that he is related to the woman or an employee designated to drive the woman. One fairly typical example is female teachers at schools for the children of expats. These expat women ride with the students in the school buses to be dropped off at their homes (and to keep the students in line).

These women technically are breaking the law in most cases. As in Iraq, a work visa applies to the person employed by the company sponsoring the visa, usually the husband. If the company permits the man's family to join him, his wife and children are only allowed to reside in the country, not work. However, the Saudi authorities do not actively check whether expat women earn money teaching or running a daycare for expat children, as long as they do so quietly and invisibly. Trouble arises only if something serious happens that requires official attention.

For women like Kumud, who are well-educated and highly skilled, life as an expat wife constitutes a serious detour to her career and future ability to find work. Being a wife and mother certainly demonstrates a wide range of abilities. Unfortunately, employers place little value on homemaking. Some women are hired by international schools if they have the background to teach the subjects offered. They do not cost as much as teachers recruited from overseas and brought in with work visas. As a result, tuition fees can remain reasonable.

Kumud took a different tack. Since she already was looking after our son, she decided to open the Daffodils Preschool at our house. Thirty or so kids, mostly from Arabic countries like Egypt, Tunisia, and Jordan, signed up. This was a great initial experience for Kumud as an entrepreneur. She even invited the wife of the Indian ambassador to the Kingdom to visit the school on a few special occasions.

Troubles are much more likely while in public places. Most readers are probably aware that Saudi women are required to wear burqas, a head to toe black robe that only permits others to see the woman's eyes and hands. Sometimes, even the eyes are covered by sheer black cloth. What you might not know is that women dress like this only in public and, usually, only while in the Kingdom. Whenever Kumud hosted friends of our Saudi landlord's wife, her guests opened or removed their burqas since they knew no men were around. Under the plain black robe, they wore splendidly fashionable outfits, expensive, European styles that one might see on the better streets of New York or Paris. Saudi husbands take their wives to fancy stores to please them, since the women have so little entertainment. Also, at a certain point on every flight out of Saudi Arabia, women in burqas queue to use the restroom so they can remove the garment. On every flight to Saudi Arabia, they queue up to put it on before reaching Saudi airspace.

The dress code is not quite as strict for expats unless they are Muslim. Non-Muslim women can just wear an *abayah*, a black robe of light material that covers the woman from the neck down, including her arms. Saudi drivers always seem to be eager to look for foreign women in other vehicles who don't have to have their faces covered. It's a wonder this doesn't cause more accidents! While Saudi men typically wear white robes and the familiar head wrap, expats wear whatever is appropriate for their positions.

Viney recalls a few incidents in which we were less circumspect in our attire as we should have been upon leaving our house:

One day, we went with another Indian couple to visit Batha market in Riyadh. This market is like the downtown area of a large U.S. city, with all sorts of shops and restaurants. Expats in Riyadh tend to shop at Batha more frequently than anywhere else. Our wives were in the middle of negotiations in a shop. My friend and I were approached by *muttawa*, religious police in plain clothes but recognizable by their long beards. *Muttawa* circulate in public spaces looking for offenders of the social standards. We were just two husbands standing outside a shop, waiting for our wives to come out. The police asked in Arabic if the two ladies they were identifying belonged to us. On our confirmation, they became extremely angry. They started gesturing towards the ladies' ankles. What they meant was that my wife's ankles were exposed. The dress she was wearing was revealing a part of her body that men outside her family should never see. They ordered us to get the women out and rush to our homes as soon as possible. While the offense involved Kumud's choice in clothing, a woman's closest male relatives are held accountable for her behavior. I was in danger of being penalized with lashes for my wife's act of immodesty.

We ran inside the shop and virtually dragged our wives out. They were bewildered and wanted to know what was going on. We told them to leave the negotiations and just get out. We had to immediately rush home. Although they did not understand the reason, they complied. Indeed, it was clear that something was terribly wrong, but our sudden insistence that we leave Batha was terribly confusing to them. While all this was happening, the *muttawas* were observing us. They ensured we were back in our cars. Once inside the cars, we could explain to our spouses what had happened. Only then did they fully realize the seriousness of the situation and the reason for urgency.

A similar incident regarding the dress code for males is still very fresh in my memory. During our stay in Riyadh, one of our family friends who worked for the Food and Agriculture Organization of the United Nations visited us from Delhi. On the day of his departure, I took him to Riyadh airport during the early morning hours. I was wearing shorts and a T-shirt. Since I was not going to get out of the car, I decided to go to the airport as is. Maybe the heat muddled my thinking, or I was just being lazy.

Once at the Riyadh airport, I bade goodbye to my friend from within the car, and he went inside the terminal. I was about to pull away when a Saudi woman opened the back door and asked me in Arabic to take her to an address in Riyadh. She thought my car was a taxi. As soon as she saw how I was dressed, especially the shorts, she virtually ran from the car to a nearby *muttawa*. Even though the incident occurred as a result of the woman's mistake, I knew right away I was in trouble and if caught could end up in jail. The moment I realized she was rushing towards a *muttawa*, I just took off. That was perhaps the fastest I have ever driven in Saudi Arabia. I was looking at the rear view mirror all the while home to spot if a police car was chasing me. Even if one was, I was driving so fast, it would have had little chance of catching up with me.

I got home, 51 kilometers from the airport, in 22 minutes. I knew I had escaped a big disaster. Even though there are unmanned radar set-ups to monitor drivers' speed all along the airport road, I was mentally prepared to get a big ticket in the mail in lieu of whatever the consequences would have been if I was stopped on the road; at a minimum, I would have been sent to jail. Luckily, I did not get a ticket. It was definitely quite an escape and taught us how important it was to always dress in accordance with the cultural and religious expectations in Saudi Arabia.

One of the more entertaining aspects of life in the Kingdom involves observing how Saudis handle the restrictions that had caused us some terrifying incidents. Since men are not supposed to see unrelated women unless they are covered up, some accommodations must be made in business establishments. We witnessed a very amusing sight in a mall food court where a veiled woman was trying to eat spaghetti without showing her mouth in public. To avoid these difficulties, fast food restaurants typically have a dining area for families and a separate area for men eating alone or with other men. That way, women do not have to worry about accidentally unveiling while eating. Also, some shopping malls and stores are strictly for women. However, given how covered women are, the *muttawa* are always alert to men dressing in burqas so they can visit these places and look at women.

Hair salons are strictly female territory, but Kumud witnessed an interesting little subterfuge. A young woman was dropped off at a salon by her brother. The brother drove off rather than sit around waiting for her to have her hair done. Once he was clearly gone, another car pulled up, and the woman left the salon and got in the car. A bit later, the woman was dropped off and was all set when her brother returned to pick her up. Since her head was covered, the brother would not have noticed that she had nothing done to her hair while he was gone. An appointment at the salon was just a ruse for his sister to spend time with her boyfriend.

Viney had the biggest scare of all toward the end of our stay:

I can never forget that sunny day in February 1989 in Riyadh. I had just dropped off my daughter and a few kids of our friends at the Indian Embassy School and was on my way back from the school to my office. The time was around 8:30 a.m. At a traffic light, I started to cross the intersection when the light turned green. I was midway through the crossing when an Egyptian man just appeared in front of my car, trying to cross the road on a red light. Though I tried to stop the car with all my might applied to the brakes, there was no chance to avoid him. The car bonnet hit him hard. His knee was dislocated. The police came in no time. The man was taken to the National Medical Center, which happened to be just across the road.

I was asked by the police to accompany them to the hospital in the police car. After the injured man was admitted to the hospital, the police took me to jail without ascertaining what had happened. My car was still there at the accident site on the side of the road. Here I was, locked up in jail within 30 minutes of the accident. Kumud and my office had no clue where I was whatsoever. I was allowed to make two calls: one to my office, and the other to my home.

I stayed in the jail for two uneasy nights. The experience was horrible but also very interesting. They kept over thirty men in a small room. No difference was made between drug traffickers, murderers, and people like me who had been involved in traffic accidents. Only a handful understood a little bit of English. Even so, I managed to understand parts of the stories from men incarcerated for serious crimes. I had one small blanket and food that was difficult to eat. Fortunately, my wife was allowed to send food in the evenings. If my company had not sprang into action and obtained the governor's approval in two days to get me released on bail, I could easily have been stuck there for at least a week, if not several weeks.

The whole experience gave me a good glimpse of legal process in Saudi Arabia. As noted earlier, the legal system of Saudi Arabia is based on sharia, Islamic law derived from the Quran and the Sunnah (the traditions) of the Prophet Mohammed. Sources of sharia also include scholarly consensus developed over the years after Mohammad's death. Interpretation by judges in Saudi Arabia of how to apply sharia is influenced by the medieval texts of the literalist Hanbali school of jurisprudence.

Once I was out of jail, I approached the injured Egyptian man in the hospital to discuss an out-of-court settlement. His demand was 100,000 Saudi rials (US$1 = 3.75 rials). The auto insurance company refused to oblige his demand. My fear grew that I would face punishment according to sharia precepts. I feared I might be punished with eye for an eye or, in this case, knee for a knee justice. The Friday mosque in downtown Riyadh is the location, after prayers, set aside for publicly punishing convicted criminals with lashes, mutilation, etc. Everyone is urged to attend to create deference to the law. The serious problem with this system is that punishments for minor infractions are so severe. On the other hand, justice is quite swift. After three months, the court gave the verdict. Much to my relief, they asked me to pay the injured man compensation of 7,500 rials, only 7.5 percent of what he had demanded. The best result of this mess concluding was I was now able to travel again. During the three months while the case was under review, I was not allowed to travel out of the country. My passport was held, making me a prisoner of the Kingdom, albeit a prisoner outside a prison.

Muslims are forbidden to drink alcohol. Ironically, the English word "alcohol" comes from Arabic. Anyway, Saudi Arabia is dry; beer, wine, and liquor are completely banned. The authorities are so concerned about anything that causes intoxication of any kind that they even ban nutmeg because in large enough quantities it is a hallucinogenic. Expats can drive to Bahrain or fly to Dubai or Abu Dhabi to imbibe if they have a multiple re-entry visa. However, many expats find it is less expensive and somewhat fun to make wine at home from commercially available pure grape juice. We intended to consume any wine we made within our own family or, at best, with a few friends. Viney got a recipe from one of his doctor friends. The ingredients, yeast and sugar along with the juice, are readily available. Large containers needed for water on longer drives were plentiful. Viney started the process of winemaking at home,

71

and we waited the four to six weeks for fermentation. The first batch of red wine was absolutely great. We relished the taste, and more importantly our innovativeness. There is a cardinal principle that forbidden fruits taste better. That principle applied even more so in this case, since we had a chance to share our prohibited beverage with friends and they just loved it. We immediately established a routine of making a few bottles of wine every month.

Little did we realize the danger to us engaging in this activity. One day, we were told that a person who was casually known to us had been jailed. He was given many lashes and then deported. His crime: making wine at home for personal use. The day we heard this news, we were scared to our core and immediately destroyed the few wine bottles that were already fermented and dumped the new batch that we had recently started. There is no way we could take any chance after this scary news. Looking back, we now realize the gravity of the situation. If any of our friends had mentioned our winemaking inadvertently or just as part of friendly banter to their friends, and if the information spread until it was leaked to the wrong person, we could have been in a very big mess.

The funny thing is that even though the ban on alcohol is strictly followed officially, the upper strata of society, in particular members of the royal family, are known for drinking liquor. And expats weren't the only people who drove on the long causeway to neighboring Bahrain to enjoy alcoholic drinks; Saudi citizens were just as likely to be making the trip.

In Saudi Arabia, idolatry in any form is also forbidden. Their interpretation of Islamic law prohibits depictions of Allah or the gods of any other religion. This posed a problem since, as Hindus, we are used to worshipping pictures of our gods and goddesses, e.g. Krishna, Rama, etc. Kumud could not resist the temptation to smuggle representations of some of our Indian gods on her return from India when she travelled there in 1986. It was a very risky move. She could have been immediately deported back to India for this offence. In fact, we knew somebody who was deported for bringing a copy of the Bible with him. Kumud was luckier. She escaped without being caught, even though her luggage was searched. Those idols and pictures of our gods became prized

72

possessions. When we left the Kingdom in 1990, we gifted them to another Indian family, who sincerely appreciated our gesture. Looking back, we now realize how risky it was to break the law for something trivial like this or having wine. There is some rationality in making punishments severe and public for minor offenses. Would we take similar risks today? Hell no!

Before leaving Riyadh in 1990, we enjoyed a rather unique experience. When our son was about five years old, he asked why his name was so unlike the names of the other Indian children. Viney explained that he had been named after the leader of Iraq, where he had been born. Our son thought about that and said he would like to see this man for whom he was named. Although we knew nothing much would come of it, Viney wrote a letter to Saddam Hussein explaining that our son was interested in the man whose name he shared and wanted to meet him. We forgot about the letter until about six months later, when we received a call from the Iraqi Embassy. The ambassador wished to speak with us and invited us to the embassy. Little did we realize that a simple letter sent to Saddam Hussein's attention by ordinary post some six months back was the reason we had been asked to attend this meeting. We were understandably concerned that perhaps we had raised the ire of a man increasingly known as a dictator. It turned out that President Hussein was inviting our family to visit Iraq for a week as his personal, official guests and at state expense so our son could visit the country where he was born.

We were not able to accept the invitation immediately and had some reservations about doing so, but soon enough we arrived in Baghdad in June 1989 as guests of President Saddam Hussain. We toured palaces and museums and were treated like royalty. Unfortunately, the President was in Cairo that week, so our son was not able to meet him. However, during this return visit to Iraq, we went with our son to show him the hospital where he was born. Sadly, we found that the hospital had been converted into a prisoner of war camp for Iranian soldiers captured during the war that had just ended, only to be followed by another in 1990.

The Iraqi Information Minister told us before our return flight to the Kingdom that we would always be welcome to visit Iraq as guests of the state. We simply had to get in touch with the Iraqi embassy wherever we were in the world, and the staff would make all of the arrangements for our return visit as honored guests of the President. We never had an opportunity to take advantage of this generous offer. It is just as well. We can't describe the feeling one has of being connected to infamy as a result of serendipity and eccentricity.

After we immigrated to Canada a short while later in February 1990, the Gulf War involving Iraq's illegal occupation of Kuwait took place. Saddam Hussein's name was forever tarnished. Our son decided to abandon that dreaded name and adopted a new name. Now his passport identifies him as Varun Kaushal, although his Canadian nationality documents still list Saddam as his middle name. Fortunately, he has not shown any signs of emulating the man for whom he was named in any way. At least not yet!

We have kept the letter as memento of this adventure. Photographs of the letter is reproduced in the Appendix.

It is funny how destiny plays a role in our lives. We were at a social dinner in Saudi sometime in 1988 when an Indian couple, the Mehras, who were friends of ours, suddenly announced that they were immigrating to Canada. We still had one or two years remaining of our stay in the Kingdom. Our friends' decision made us curious as to how we could immigrate to Canada. As we mentioned earlier, our visit to London and Paris had planted the seed that we ought to consider moving to Europe. Now, the seed was transplanted to North America.

After our various adventures negotiating religion-based strictures on our lives, we were very anxious to get out of Saudi Arabia and reside in the West. We applied for landed immigrant status to Canada in July 1988. Even though we were told it usually takes 18 months, we were eager to find a way to speed up the process. A Somali colleague suggested entering Canada by train from the U.S. and applying for refugee status. If approved, an entire family could immigrate. Although we had concerns about violence against non-Sikhs in Punjab at the time, we doubted that would sway the Canadian authorities, given we hadn't lived in Punjab in years. Besides, asking to be declared a refugee after already submitting a landed immigrant application sounded much too risky and uncertain.

While we waited for a response to our application, a doctor friend and Viney obtained visas to visit the U.S. They flew into Washington, D.C., and stayed with the doctor's friend in Virginia. Aside from evaluating options for immigrating to USA, Viney took the opportunity to visit universities in Boston, Philadelphia, and elsewhere to see about entering an MBA or Ph.D. program. However, he was told that he would have to take the GMAT exam to apply for business programs. That wasn't going to speed our exit from the Kingdom, although it did encourage Viney to take the GMAT in Dammam when he returned to Saudi. This turned out to be quite beneficial.

In July 1989, on an extended trip to India, we visited some astrologers for answers regarding when we could move to Canada. One said point blank you will not get your visas. A really famous one, Shakuntala Devi, a world famous mathematician who charged a rather high fee, was supposed to excel at drawing astrological charts and fixing the stars when doing so. She said we would get our visas if we fixed our stars through her at that very moment after paying the required high fee. A couple of days after our meeting, we saw in the newspapers that her house was burgled and stripped of anything worthwhile. We had to wonder why she did not draw her own star chart and see this disaster would befall her. We paid her a lot of money, but could we trust her?

Another astrologer said we should go to a lake in Chandigarh and feed the fish at 7 a.m. every day for half an hour. That would speed up the visa process. We did that for about five weeks. Educated, rational, logical people, but when anxiety takes over, we were willing to try anything. Anything other than just being patient and let the matter take its own course at its own pace. Whether it did any good for our visa application, the fish got fed and we had some quiet moments to start our days. Perhaps giving us a task like that helped the wait time go by faster, even if it did not make the visa processing faster.

Eventually, there was nothing to do but let the matter take its own course. As it turned out, we were approved for immigration to Canada in December 1989. We had not planned for a decision in our favor. Canada has a point-based system for skilled people interested in moving there. Our anxiety and desperate actions arose from a belief that we would not have enough points. Luckily, we were wrong. As landed immigrants, we would be able to become Canadian citizens after three years if all went well. This was a big change of plans for us, since taking advantage of this opportunity meant giving up our Indian nationality forever. We decided to take the risk, just as we had always done.

If one is being kind and positive, overlooking the worst aspects, the Kingdom is a unique country offering many chances to explore one's faith, principles, and tolerance. It makes one evaluate one's senses of honor, duty, and justice. Since so much is written that criticizes Saudi Arabia, we would much rather focus on how our experience living there shaped our perspectives and enriched our thinking. What lessons did we learn during our time in Saudi Arabia?

- *Social change comes slowly.* The society in the Kingdom has been too closed off from outside influences for many citizens to realize the alternatives. The country is opening up, but the pace is going in half-steps due to the immense influence of conservatives and the power of the *muttawa*.
- *Justice can exist even under legal structures that are wildly different.* While in any foreign country, and especially in the Middle East, the first rule is to stay clear of legal issues at any cost. It is easier to run afoul of a law as an expat or traveler than in your home country because the reasoning behind laws varies greatly from one place to the next. Sharia and the kinds of punishments used might seem scary, and one may wonder if implementation is consistent. However, chances are you will likely receive fair treatment.
- *Do not insist your way of thinking is right.* Religious intolerance for anything but Islam is entrenched throughout Saudi society for very good reasons: it is the birthplace of Islam and guardian of two of the three most holy sites in Islam. One does not have to agree with intolerance to accept that others can be intolerant.

The principle of sovereignty dictates that a country has the right to decide what is permissible and what is not. As the saying goes: "When in Rome, do as the Romans." That is not to say one cannot politely object or point out tolerant alternatives.

- *Understanding a culture includes appreciating its limitations.* Saudi Arabia has far more expats than citizens. Most of the expats, however, are construction workers, maids, and others brought from South and Southeast Asia. Even westerners and people like Viney are brought in because of the severe lack of motivation and training among Saudis. The confluence of oil wealth and religious restrictions has created a unique situation. All of the labor hired from overseas, plus exchange programs, especially for teachers, provides a new cultural awareness. The local dress code, especially for women, is quite conservative, but it isn't too far removed from ideals of modesty in other countries. Just think of the impact of virtually no entertainment. The Kingdom has no movie theaters, almost no stage theaters, restrictions on television programming, and dependency on shows from Egypt and other places with production facilities. Even Chinese citizens can watch American films, see plays, and watch a range of television shows.

Viney's Saudi Arabian Resident Card

Saudi-Bahrain Causeway 1987
with Dr. Mhatre Family

Kumud in Kashmiri dress
Fashion Show
Riyadh, Saudi Arabia 1987

Glimpse of Saudi life for ladies
in Riyadh 1986

All five brothers with Father
Sabha, India 1986

Third Interlude:
Bahrain, Cyprus, and Greece (1986-90)

"There are no foreign lands. It is the traveler only who is foreign."
Robert Louis Stevenson

We drove to Manama, the capital of Bahrain, from Riyadh with our family friends from Riyadh. The King Fahd Causeway was completed in 1986, and we were among the first few families that took this fascinating new road and bridge combination. Bahrain is the name of the largest island in an archipelago in the Arabian Gulf (aka Persian Gulf), across from Dammam in Saudi Arabia's Eastern Province. The causeway is 25 kilometers (16 miles) long and is made up of a series of bridges, roadways, and artificial embankments and islands. The border between the two kingdoms is located on two connected, artificial islands called Passport Island. This island contains the immigration and customs stations, as well as restaurants and mosques for travelers going in both directions.

Like Iraq, Bahrain has a majority Shi'a population, but the ruling family is Sunni. This has caused some tensions, particularly when the Shiites protested during the Arab Spring. However, the government is relatively progressive, with an elected assembly and women gaining the right to vote in 2002. Women also are not required to be veiled, which is rather startling after living in Saudi Arabia.

The territory originally had 33 islands, but the government has built 51 man-made islands. Most people only think of oil and Iran when talking about the Gulf. Ornithologists and marine biologists, however, know the region has much more to offer. About 220 species of birds live or transit through the islands, most spectacularly greater flamingos that live in the shallows around the coast. The waters host many rare sea creatures, like the green turtle and dugong, a relative of Florida's manatees. Divers are drawn to the coral reefs and clear waters.

The intention of building the causeway was to strengthen relations between the two countries. While that may indeed have been the result, the causeway is primarily used by Saudi citizens and expats as a means of going somewhere to drink. Aside from a few architecturally interesting bridges and buildings, there is not much to see in Bahrain. The island of Bahrain is mostly flat, rising to one small escarpment in the center. Since it is home to the United States' Fifth Fleet, large areas are off limits. So, people visit Manama to go to hotels and bars to legally drink alcohol. There are also a few liquor stores. They are prohibited from selling to Muslims, but Muslims know well enough to dress in Western-style clothing if they want to purchase from these shops.

Given that so many Saudis go there to drink, Passport Island can be difficult to navigate on the return trip. Saudis do their best to be sober before attempting to go home. More than a few probably stop in the restaurant for coffee, followed by a trip to the mosque to give the alcohol time to leave their bloodstreams. All in all, we enjoyed a pleasant break from the highly regimented life of Saudi Arabia, though only for a few days. We were able to enjoy a few beers while there without breaking any laws.

We visited Cyprus for one week during the summer of 1987. Cyprus is the third largest island in the Mediterranean Sea. The country is located south of Turkey, east of Greece's island of Crete, and west of Syria and Lebanon. The island looks a bit like a turkey drumstick. The northeast third of the island (the bone part of the drumstick) claims to be a separate country called the Turkish Republic of Northern Cyprus, but only Turkey recognizes its independence. Like many parts of the Mediterranean, including southern Italy, Tunisia, and Alexandria in Egypt, Greeks settled in Cyprus at least 25 centuries ago. Greece and Turkey have had a long rivalry dating to Greece's subjugation by the Ottoman Empire, the War of Greek Independence in the 1820s, and the expulsion of Greek-speaking citizens from their ancient homes in western Asia Minor after World War I.

Turks had moved to the island during Ottoman times, but the majority of residents remained Greek. In the 1950s, when it was a British colony, the Cypriot Turks wanted the island to become part of Turkey, the nearest country. The Greek Cypriot majority wanted to become part of Greece. Great Britain instead granted Cyprus independence in 1960. In 1974, the Greeks in the government attempted a coup d'état to force Cyprus to become part of Greece. Turkey invaded the north of the island. After years of stalemate and the displacement of many Cypriots based on what language they spoke, the north declared its independence. Due to the division of the island, there are political issues that remain sensitive. Also, since the Turks have a culture rooted in Islam, there are some religious rules that must be observed when in the northern half of the island.

This was a wonderful vacation for the family. Nicosia, the capital, is located in the interior near the dividing line with the renegade area. Like most tourists, we went to Limassol, the second largest city in the country. Limassol is located in the south of the country and contains wonderful beaches and excellent restaurants. It is an outstanding place to relax. The city and rest of the island are full of cultural monuments. Cyprus has been important for millennia as a source of copper. In fact, the word "copper" is derived from the Latin word for the island. As a result, the island hosts many Neolithic settlements and classical Greek and Roman monuments. One notable visit was to see a statue of Aphrodite. The Greek goddess of love and beauty is said to have emerged from the foam of a wave on a shell that landed on the shore of Cyprus.

As visitors to Cyprus, we were free to wear any Western-style clothing we liked. The Greeks are used to scantily-clad tourists, so they care little how people dress, while the Turks tend to be a bit more conservative. We had an issue regarding what to wear since we were on the Greek side but had been so used to dressing modestly. We created the right balance of clothing between conservative and moderate. We wore swimwear frequently, knowing full well this freedom was going to be short-lived. However, we also knew we should not get too used to it before returning to the Kingdom.

One incident that is engraved in our memory occurred while we were travelling to northern Cyprus. We had a rental car. By oversight, we crossed into the Turkish side of the town. The line that divides Greek Cyprus from the Turkish side is managed by a United Nations Peacekeeping Force. We don't know how, but the border patrol did not stop us, and we were in the middle of the Turkish portion of the island. It could have been very serious if we were not there as a family. Some soldiers saw two little kids in a rental car from Limassol and escorted us back to the border. We shudder to think if jail was in order for such border dodgers, but luckily our kids saved us from whatever punishment there would have been.

Once we were approved to move to Canada, we decided to fly to our new home via Athens so we could visit that city for a couple of days and begin the transition from the strictures we were under in Saudi Arabia. We left on February 1, 1990, on the next stage of our odyssey. We were entering an uncertain phase of our lives as new immigrants to Canada, so this break in Greece was a God-sent gift. We wanted to make the best of it, having none of the baggage of company work and Saudi rules to worry about.

We had an extensive tour of Athens and saw the National Archaeological Museum, the Agora (the central market full of local shoppers), Mount Lycabettus, which gives a panoramic view of the city, the city center, and the Panathinaiko Olympic Stadium, built entirely of marble in 1896 for the first modern Olympics. Of course, almost everyone has seen a picture of the Acropolis crowned by the ruins of the illustrious Parthenon. Finally seeing it up close was a marvel. We also learned that Athenians enjoy entertainments of many kinds. We were told Athens had 120 theaters and 130 cinemas. The Greek people love to sing and dance.

It was wonderful getting exposed to the very open Greek culture, a big change from Saudi Arabia. It was hard to imagine that we were leaving behind all the religious restrictions and entering a new phase of life full of freedom, equal work opportunities for both sexes, religious toleration, and an open society. And after nine years in the Middle East, Kumud was all set to move from the life of a homemaker to working as a professional again. We had made a wise decision to stop in Athens to be refreshed in preparation for our upcoming life settling in Canada. The whole family enjoyed this short vacation against the backdrop of apprehensions about moving to North America and a radically new environment.

Even on these short ventures into countries, we have found valuable lessons and more evidence to support lessons previously learned:

- *One religion can be interpreted and practiced in many ways.* We are so used to speaking of Christianity, Islam, Hinduism, Buddhism, etc., as though every person who identifies with one of these major religions practices his faith in the same way. Similarly, when we identify a country as being Muslim or Christian, we assume that means the same thing for every country so identified. Nothing could be further from the truth. Different Islamic countries interpret the requirements of Islam differently, particularly with regard to the treatment and liberty of women, but also other aspects such as the sale of alcohol or obligations during prayer times. It is simply wrong to think that Islam means the same to every Muslim or every Muslim country, just as it is wrong to say that Christianity means the same to every Christian or every Christian country.
- *Always be vigilant about where you are going.* It was surprisingly simple for us to accidentally wander into the Turkish enclave in Cyprus. We were fortunate to have found the right people to turn us around. On the other hand, Viney knew exactly where he was going and why when he flew to Kuwait and took that long road trip to Baghdad. Who knows which is smarter: deliberately entering a country at war, or erroneously driving into a breakaway territory?
- *Gradual transitions help prepare you for the next stage.* Athens was a wonderful break away from highly fundamentalist Saudi Arabia. Despite a whirlwind tour given the shortness of our stay, we still could recharge our batteries in a free country. We didn't have this luxury moving from India to Iraq or Iraq to Saudi; the change in cultures was abrupt, and a bit overwhelming.

On way to Vishnu Devi Temple with Megha
Jammu - Kashmir 1989

Athens, Greece 1990
End route to Canada

Canada (1990-94)

"Man cannot discover new oceans unless he has the courage to lose sight of the shore."
Andre Gide

In Saudi Arabia and Iraq, we knew we weren't going to be staying in those countries. There was no chance we could immigrate, even if we had wanted. The whole time we lived in those countries, we knew we were expats. We would be returning to India at some point. All of that changed when we decided to follow our friends' lead and apply to immigrate to Canada. And the choice became a reality when we received approval in December 1989 to become permanent residents of Canada. Many of our Indian friends in Saudi had been encouraged by our example and were at various stages of their own immigration applications to Canada, just as we had been encouraged by our friends. After packing and preparing, we said goodbye to the Kingdom for the last time and set off via our stay in Athens for a couple of days, and then to Toronto via Montreal.

February 3, 1990, was the cold and blustery day we landed in Montreal. We can never forget that day. It was easily the most important day in our lives, other than the day we married and the days when our children and grandchildren were born. All of the passengers applauded the flight crew for landing the plane safely after the long flight. We privately wanted to believe we were being welcomed to our new home in Canada. There was heavy snowfall when we landed. Everything was white and beautiful. We were so happy to be greeted with the snow, even though we never got out of the plane to touch it. We still had the last leg of the flight from Montreal to Toronto.

The entire flight time from Athens to Toronto via Montreal was 14 hours. The immigration officials at Toronto checked our landing papers (a sample is reproduced in the Appendix), greeted us warmly, stamped our passports as landed immigrants, gave us information about local hotels and said, "Welcome to Canada." They spent about half an hour explaining everything we needed to do about finding a hotel, signing up for social and health insurance, and taking care of all the actions needed to settle in our new home. The official did not care about the details of where we would be staying or what we would be doing next, unlike passport control people when you are just visiting a country. When we left the airport terminal, the snow was falling like cats and dogs that momentous day in our lives. It was quite fitting. We were going to have to acclimate ourselves to our new home quickly. We were leaving a part of us in India forever. Before long, we were going to be Canadian nationals. We were going to lose our Indian passports, but not our Indian identity.

Landed immigrants are allowed to import all of their possessions to Canada duty-free. We had almost everything shipped, including ten or twelve Persian rugs. Shipping in this case means literally sending everything on a ship, not shipping like at the post office. We knew we would have to wait three months for our household goods to arrive. In the meantime, we had two suitcases each of clothes and personal items.

The Mehra family, our friends who had emigrated one year before us from Riyadh and motivated us to apply for immigration to Canada, picked us up. They lived in their own home near the airport. We had been quite surprised when our friends told us they had bought their own home within a year of arriving in Toronto. Of course, they had brought a lot of money saved from working in Saudi Arabia, so they had been able to put a down payment on a house so soon. We were lucky we had friends to help us. Otherwise, we would have had to move into a hotel on the day of our arrival. That was not a pleasant thought, considering we already were thinking of Canada as our new home. It was much easier to maintain that sentiment staying in a house. The Mehras also helped us adapt and use the information the immigration official had explained when we were weary from the long trip. They gave us guidance on signing up for healthcare and all of the other social programs available to Canadians and landed immigrants.

Ten days after our arrival, we moved into our own apartment in North York, a suburb on the north side of Toronto. We had some difficulty in renting. The problem was that neither one of us had a job at that point. Finally, a considerate landlord offered us an apartment, provided that we paid six months' rent in advance. We understood the need for the advance and were grateful to find a place of our own. Given where we had lived previously, we had not really encountered many Jewish people. Now we had a Jewish landlord who, by renting to us, showed us that diversity teaches one that people from different backgrounds are still just people with the full range of human strengths and frailties. It reinforced our feeling that we had chosen well in deciding to immigrate to Canada.

Kumud was hired for a job with the National Trust Bank (now Scotia Bank) about ten days later, just three weeks after our arrival. Our landlord told her that the place where he did his banking was hiring people. Of course, Kumud had experience working for an Indian bank, but she was not aware of banking procedures in Canada. She completed the application and was interviewed. It went something like this:

"Can you differentiate between the various Canadian coins?"

"Yes. In learning to shop, it was necessary to figure out the coins in order to pay and to make sure I received the correct change."

"That's wonderful that you picked that up so quickly. Now, you don't have any local experience, do you? You have never worked for a Canadian bank."

"No, my family just immigrated, so I have not worked in Canada. But if you give me a job, I will have local experience. Moreover, I worked in a bank in India for five years."

The manager was impressed with her reasoning and hired her. The odd thing is that Viney also found interviewers always asked, "Do you have Canadian experience?" For a country that is so welcoming to immigrants, it is quite unfair for employers to ask this question. Unless the immigrant previously had a work visa for Canada, the answer is going to be "No." Most new immigrants can't gain local experience unless someone hires them, and if employers won't hire people without local experience, immigrants are in a no-win situation. New Canadian residents need the opportunity to learn local business practices, as well as earn money. Kumud was fortunate the bank manager understood her response and recognized she was sincere.

February 21 was Kumud's first day of work. Since we didn't have a car, she was going to have to take a one-hour bus ride each way for her job, changing buses once. So on that first day, she left our apartment for the bus stop. Within minutes, she was running back from the bus stop.

Viney asked, "What happened? Why are you back?"

Kumud replied frantically, "I left the apartment and completely forgot to put on an *abayah*!"

Viney couldn't help but laugh. "Kumud, we are in Canada now, not Saudi. Remember? You don't need to wear an *abayah* anymore when you go out."

Kumud settled into her job and excelled. She learned Canadian banking practices and her duties fully within a few months. Just as elsewhere, Kumud was a dedicated, effective employee. Within two years, she was promoted to an investment officer position.

Varun was only five, so he was not in full day school yet. We were looking for day care or some other place for him to be with other kids. Part of the need for this also was that Viney had to take Varun with him while applying and interviewing for jobs. Even though Varun was respectful, Viney had the impression that the employers had a negative reaction to Varun tagging along. Perhaps they wondered what we would do for Varun if his father got a job, since neither parent would be home then. Fortunately, we found a half-day school for children Varun's age and were able to arrange for people to take him in the rest of the day. Megha and Varun enjoyed their schools and were happy to be in Canada. For them, life had started after having spent their lives as expat kids in the Middle East.

Viney was offered a job selling vacuum cleaners. Even today, companies that sell products like cars, insurance, and large appliances are always looking for fresh employees, even ones like Viney who have no sales experience. Viney decided to turn down the offer. It wasn't right for him. He can see himself now still selling vacuum cleaners or some other product, given the limited avenues for promotion. That would not have been an eventful path.

Indeed, the next job offer turned out to be a golden opportunity for someone like Viney, who enjoys challenges, learning, and responsibility. Not only does he value them on their own, but also because when one excels in those areas, superiors notice and provide even greater chances to be challenged and learn, to take on greater responsibility. A copy of Viney's first job advertisement is reproduced in the appendix.

A week or so after Kumud began working, Viney secured a job as junior payroll clerk with CM Brake, a brake pad manufacturer that was in the middle of being bought by Tenneco Automotive, a large U.S. company famous for making Monroe shocks, Walker exhausts, and many other auto parts brands. The timing could not have been better to become an employee. The guy responsible for hiring at CM Brake had immigrated from India decades earlier and knew it was important to get a job. Although the job was too junior for Viney, given his experience, this was a foot in the door and, more importantly, the right door. Within two months, he was promoted to human resources manager under the company based in Chicago. Now we had two respectable jobs, and the corresponding respectable incomes. We felt we had really started our settlement in Canada. Fortune had even more in store for us, because we discovered this job put Viney in the right place at the right time and laid the groundwork for our move to the United States eventually.

One can imagine all of the secondary issues involved with resettling in a completely new environment. They can be both fun and trying. For example, we had our first taste of garage sales within three weeks of arrival. It was an unexpected and pleasant experience. Some people were moving to Italy, and rather than ship their furniture and many other household items, they were selling them at "fire sale" prices. We found a sofa set and a bedroom set for C$150 each. In fact, we grabbed everything we could that we needed. Remember, our household goods were still in transit and would be for a couple of months. For that reason, and because we were still getting jobs, we did not want to waste money. This garage sale was perfect. And we became hooked on garage sales for some time. We even placed a sticker on our car that read "My Car Stops At Every Garage Sale."

Speaking of the car, we purchased a late-model Honda Accord. The vehicle provided us with fairly reliable service for three years before breaking down completely. Our international driver licenses were valid for six months before we had to get Canadian licenses. Getting a Canadian driving license is a big challenge. Most newcomers fail the test many times due to one issue or another.

Primarily, it seemed the examiners wanted immigrants to get more experience driving Canadian streets and highways. Sometimes they failed people for flimsy reasons. Although Viney had driven in Iraq and Saudi Arabia for eight years, he failed three times before finally getting a Canadian driving license by the end of 1990.

The change from our life in Saudi was dramatic. In the Kingdom, we wore shackles made from our anxiety about making sure we weren't breaking any regulations every time we went out in public. We spent some time getting used to the sudden freedom from Middle Eastern restrictions, as Kumud's *abayah* incident demonstrates. A clear change was our ability to start going to Hindu and Sikh temples. Saudi provided for Muslim worship only, and Iraq was almost the same, except for the Christian communities. We felt Canadian culture was fertile ground in which we could grow. We just had to work for what we wanted.

One effort along these lines was Viney's decision in December 1990 to join the MBA program offered by the University of Toronto while doing his full-time job. It was a big commitment to balance job, studies, and family. Age was not on his side either. He was 39 years old. Then again, is there any age too old to stop improving oneself? It put the onus on Kumud to fill in the gaps, especially with the children, even though she was working full-time and had housework and cooking to do. The sacrifice was necessary because every employer wanted Viney to have a local qualification.

Fortunately, he had taken the Graduate Management Admission Test, or GMAT, in Dammam, Saudi Arabia, the year before and had scored well. If he hadn't, waiting to take it in Canada would have delayed his admission by at least a year. As it was, the courses would take three years. The program administrators liked that Viney had so much international experience. Having taken that first risky job in Iraq was paying off. But once Viney completed this second MBA (after the one from India) in 1994, we found that this local degree would pay off a thousand times over in the next 25 years. For starters, with his upgraded qualifications, the company, which by now had become a Tenneco Automotive subsidiary, included Viney in a global reengineering project, with extensive travel to the U.S. and Europe.

Kumud established herself as a successful banker and within two years was promoted to a position as officer. She also upgraded her qualifications with computer courses and other skills. While Viney was balancing his responsibilities on many fronts, Kumud was an anchor to keep everything about the family together. We were not able to socialize much, given the demands on our time, but those three years provided a great foundation for the future.

The children loved the change from the Middle East and embraced North American culture quickly. They made many local friends and loved the experience. Before long, we could hear changes in their accents. Peer pressure became visible in what they liked or didn't like. These changes made us go to Indian temples more often to keep them grounded in Indian values. We wanted the best of both worlds for them. We also enrolled them in Hindi classes to learn our language and continued to celebrate festivals like Diwali and Holi. Last, we made sure we had a good supply of Indian movies for the family to watch. However, we did not discourage Megha and Varun from integrating into Canadian culture. The children became particularly excited celebrating Halloween, one of several totally new holidays to them. They also enjoyed Christmas, as did their parents, because the lights made everything so cheerful and special. We also started celebrating Easter traditions and marked Canada Day every July 1st.

We bought our first home in North America in July 1991, within 18 months of our arrival in Canada. Our interest in purchasing a house was spurred on by our friends from Riyadh, who had taken us to their house from the airport when we first arrived in Toronto. We thought that since they had found a house and arranged a mortgage within one year of immigrating, we should be able to do the same. Although it took us a bit longer, getting our new home in such a short time was quite an achievement.

The property was a beautiful, semi-detached home in Thornhill, a prestigious northern suburb of Toronto. We still remember the price in 1991 was C$256,000. The location was exceptional. The children could walk to school. A subway station was convenient, giving us easy access to most of the metropolitan Toronto area. Viney was about 15 minutes' drive from his job, and Kumud now only needed one bus and 45 minutes to get to work. We really loved the home ownership experience in North America, even though it meant having a mortgage, paying for utilities, paying rather high taxes, and the other responsibilities of owning property. The costs drove us to live paycheck to paycheck and to become landlords. It is common for Canadian homes to have a basement with a separate entrance. That makes the space ideal for renting. About the only thing that requires sorting is deciding when your tenant can use the washer and dryer, given they had to share the use of our set.

When an unusually frightening event happens in one's life, the experience seems to find its own permanent part of the memory. Even the slightest reminder will awaken it and bring back the same emotions one felt when the incident occurred. On one unfortunate day in 1993, Kumud was working in her post at National Trust Bank. The day seemed quite normal. A customer wearing a hood on his head seemed quite normal. However, when he walked up to a teller, he pulled out a gun, pointed it at her, and asked for all of the money in her drawer. She handed over the cash. She was trembling, but silent. Then other employees saw her almost fall down in a faint and suddenly knew about the robbery. The hooded man told everyone not to move. He went around to each teller station and took all of the money. Banks keep the minimum necessary to transact business out front, so the employees knew they weren't handing over much. Besides, insurance covers losses due to robbery. Tellers and all other bank employees know the only thing to do is hand over the money as calmly as possible.

The robber was unaware that the manager had pushed the emergency button for the police. Nonetheless, he ran out just before police arrived and managed to get away. Everyone was left shocked. The police said not to use the phone. They took the fingerprints of all employees to be able to narrow down the robber to earlier customers who'd left. Kumud finally was able to call Viney after two hours. The crime was all over the news. Of course, there is nothing one can do when one happens to be at the wrong place at the wrong time. Ever since, Kumud has always been quick to notice similar incidents in the news.

We were busy balancing all of our jobs, family, and Viney's schoolwork. Kumud began to have health issues from the stress in 1993-94. In December 1993, we went to a mall. Kumud had taken the regular stairs by herself. She slipped and tumbled all the way down about 30 stairs. Viney came out of a restroom and saw the crowd. He had no idea that his wife was the center of all the attention. Someone called 911. EMS came in a few minutes. She was in a lot of pain. The emergency room doctors determined there were no fractures, but she suffered bruising to her back and spine. She needed rehab, starting the next day.

The next morning, Viney was to fly to Chicago for a big presentation to the chairman and CEO of the company. Kumud insisted he go. Her mother was staying with us and could help her. It turned out the meeting with the Chairman gave Viney the visibility to be in line for a promotion to a position with the company in the USA. Kumud slowly recovered but had the added stress once Viney was offered the job in Chicago and had to be out of town a lot. In the end, Kumud came out stronger having suffered the injuries but still kept moving forward.

We were quite fortunate that Kumud's mother was living with us at that point. In 1993, Kumud was eligible for three weeks of vacation. We decided she would go to India in May 1993 to bring back Viney's father, who owned a high school in India at that time. He was 68 years old and had never been abroad or on a plane. Visiting a foreign country was a dream trip for him. Also, Kumud's mother had been approved to immigrate to Canada, so all three could travel back together. Everything went smoothly with the official business involved in leaving a country and boarding the flight. The two parents made a "Kumud sandwich", with her in the middle seat between them. The flight left.

About 15 minutes later, Viney's father remarked, "We aren't moving." He was quite apprehensive of flying

Kumud looked at him and said, "Yes, we are moving. We are in the air." Assured flying wasn't as bad as he had thought, he heaved a sigh of relief.

Next, Viney's father noticed the Western-style clothes worn by the female flight attendants. He was surprised by the clothes since he was so used to traditional Indian outfits. He asked, "What are they wearing?"

Uh oh, Kumud thought. I wear the same clothes in Canada. "Those are called skirts. They are worn at the waist down. A woman wears a blouse or sweater on top." How was he going to react when his daughter-in-law wore similar clothes to go to her job at the bank?

One of the stewardesses brought him his meal. He was pleased to see that vegetarians like him were well looked after. The remainder of the flight was uneventful, except when Kumud had to show her mother and Viney's father, separately, how to use the sit down toilets on board. For Viney's father, there were going to be many new experiences. Women's dresses and Western restrooms were just the beginning

The trio stopped in London for a week to visit Kumud's sister. Her sister and brother-in-law showed them all of the major sites and explained their history. Since British rule in India began centuries ago and only grew, the London visit had a special significance for Viney's father. He had gone to jail many times before India got its independence in 1947, protesting against British rule and injustices. In London, he was pleased to see Indians living as equals in the country of the Goraas (white people). He had a chance to interact with many native Britons and was able to discuss politics with them. While growing up in India under British rule, he could never have imagined having such discussions with any British person. To Viney's father's surprise, Kumud's sister and husband even had a Western couple as tenants in their home.

Then it was on to Toronto. Viney's father stayed for a month. During his visit, he and Viney drove to Boston and New York City, returning through Niagara Falls. He loved the experience of seeing parts of North America. For his return trip to India, we booked him on Air France. That way, we were able to make arrangements for a Pakistani friend who had been Viney's colleague in Iraq to pick him up at the Paris airport and show him around during the eight-hour layover.

Viney's father had a master's degrees in history and Indian culture. Seeing places he had read about and getting a taste of other cultures played directly to his passions. His only regret was not to have seen Chicago, where Swami Vivekananda delivered his historical speech in 1893. Still, the trip had a lasting impact. He was able to teach about his experience in morning sessions at the school he owned in India, creating a series of lectures from his memories.

Unfortunately, he died a few years later in 1996. We know he cherished the experience up to the last day of his life.

Viney's father was even contemplating immigrating to Canada. It was easy to sponsor parents' applications for residence in Canada at that time. The process took less than a year to complete. We already had the experience of sponsoring Kumud's mother. Our intention was for Kumud's mother to live with us permanently and give our children a taste of home life in India. However, she grew to miss life in India. After one and a half years with us, we said our goodbyes and, with mixed emotions, sent her back to the home she had always known.

We had continued to explore our new home whenever we could. There are many recreation activities available in metropolitan Toronto. We went to Canada's Wonderland, a lovely amusement park, every few weeks. We frequented downtown Toronto to visit the Sky Dome (now Rogers Centre) and CN Tower, pretty much the easiest landmark to find of any landmark in any city. World-famous Niagara Falls and the African Lion Safari Park, a drive-through kind of zoo, are just short drives south. Montreal wasn't too far for us to visit a few times. Having eagerly gotten to know all of the fun to be had, it was always equally fun to take people around to these places. In 1992, we also took a long car trip from Toronto to Montreal, Boston, New York, Washington, and crossing back to Canada at Niagara Falls. We took another road trip to St. Louis and Detroit to visit friends during December 1990. We figured that we should use rented cars instead of taking our own for any trips out of Toronto. We would then have a new, reliable vehicle for our excursion.

We had no trouble buying our first car in Canada, but when we needed to replace it in 1993, we had a weird experience. First of all, we were unaware that when one trades in the vehicle one has for a certain amount, that goes to the cost of the car one is purchasing. We visited a used car dealer who offered C$1000 for our car. We used that as a C$1000 deposit and made another deposit of C$1,500 in cash to buy a used Toyota Corolla priced at C$9,000. We waited one week without any car to get the new-to-us used car certified by the dealer to meet Canadian regulatory standards.

When we finally picked up our new car, we drove no more than 500 yards before smoke started coming out. We took it back immediately. The dealer refused to give us our money back. He offered to fix whatever was wrong, but we had no confidence in him by then. We had no choice but to sue the dealer in small claims court. He didn't show up on the date the matter was scheduled to be heard, so we won the judgment automatically. Once we received the judge's order, Viney took the judgment to the dealer's store. He found a big sign in the window: Business Closed. Viney went down the street to make inquiries. He found out from the dealer's neighbors that the dealer's business had declared bankruptcy and all the cars had been sold off or moved. We assumed we could never recover the judgment for our C$2500. Then a few months later, we received a call from a collection agency claiming that we owed $6500 to the bankrupt company for the faulty car, a vehicle we had left with the dealer immediately after picking it up. Viney told the caller that we were the ones owed money by the bankrupt company and we had a judge's order to prove it. That was that. Now we had no car, and we lost our deposit. It was an expensive way to learn why used car dealers are one of the least trusted groups anywhere.

A different matter of trust arose where Viney worked. Viney's company was not a union shop. By 1994, as human relations manager for three years, he had been encouraging loyalty among employees and leniency among supervisors long enough to think everyone was happy. The company held summer picnics and Christmas parties for employees that were a big hit. As far as Viney knew, management had great relations with the employees. However, one small element among the workers wanted to unionize. These few obtained support for a unionizing petition that was sent to the responsible ministry. Viney was quite surprised to receive a call informing him that the ministry had received the petition and would begin the process of an inquiry, followed by a decision to approve creation of a union or not.

Viney was upset that the amicable relations he had supported could be undermined by just a few. Neither he nor the other company managers were really anti-union, they just thought all was well. Viney knew the importance of being vigilant about how things are going among employees. He had no intelligence from any source about any discontent. Given his position, he blamed himself for not being aware of the petition. Since the ministry found everything to be in order to allow a union, the petition was granted. The workplace changed forever after the union was formed. The union, especially how it was formed, had hurt the trust that had developed.

Landed immigrants are eligible to apply and interview for citizenship after three years of continuous residence in Canada. Given how much we enjoyed adapting to our new home, jobs, and schools, we certainly wanted to take advantage of this opportunity. Just when all was getting set in Canada, the first fruit of our intention to stay ripened. Viney completed his MBA in May 1994 on schedule, thus achieving the local qualification so important to advancement. Then our family received Canadian citizenship in June 1994. Immigrants who move to Canada while leaving close family ties behind are always thinking about who else in the family would be a good candidate to immigrate also. Viney asked his oldest brother, who had been in the Indian Army, and found him the job in Iraq. He received five extra points under the Canadian immigration assessment system because he was a relative of Canadians. Viney's brother and family easily obtained landed immigrant status and moved in August 1994 to Canada where he still lives and works.

Just when Viney was obtaining his MBA, his company decided to execute a global initiative to reengineer the whole company with twenty new projects. They were looking for a director to lead the effort. Viney had already achieved ISO 9001 certification for his local Canadian unit in a very short time. That established the process for certification for as many of the 73 global units of the company as possible. Viney's achievements were recognized by the company.

When the global role opened up, Viney was chosen from a group of many very serious contenders. This was a huge jump and an honor for a human resources manager and, moreover, a recent immigrant to North America. Remember, Viney had started his job four years back as a junior payroll clerk in the company, and now he was going to be at the head office of the company, reporting to a vice president. He would be just three levels away from the CEO.

In quick order, Viney received his degree, the entire family took their oaths as new Canadian citizens, and Viney was rewarded with a big promotion as Global Director of Total Quality Management, based in Chicago from July 1994 onwards. This was another big decision for the family. The choice was to stick around in Canada and be content continuing in his human resources role or jump into the ocean of opportunities that lay waiting in the USA. Since it would only require an L1 visa, the type used for company transfers, obtaining residency would not be an issue.

We evaluated the pros and cons of moving to Chicago despite having just become Canadians. On the pro side, we knew it was a substantial opportunity that promised Viney a higher income and a better future with Tenneco Automotive. Our children would be going to well-established middle and high schools and have a greater variety of universities to consider. We knew homes were more spacious than the relatively smaller houses in Canada and provided more value for your money. On the con side, our children would lose their circle of friends, Megha for a third time. Kumud would have to reestablish herself from a career point of view. And most seriously, we were a little afraid of the unknowns lurking in a future in the U.S. So, we went to someone in Toronto who is supposed to know the future: an astrologer. The astrologer said, "You should not go. The stars do not favor this move. It will weigh heavily on Kumud's health." We were probably hoping for a different response, since that only added to our fears.

Finally, Viney called his boss, Luan Watkins, a vice president with whom we have remained in contact to this day.

Viney asked the question at the root of our concerns. "What are we to do if the job ends after the project is completed in a couple of years?"

Her response was direct, honest, and comforting. "If you take advantage of this opportunity, the company will find work for you if this job ends. You will stay in the U.S. with a job with us. End of story. We will help you get your green card, so residency will not be an issue."

Convinced by her assurances, Viney accepted the offer, defying the astrologer's prediction, and went to Chicago with Kumud for a week to evaluate the area, housing, and school districts. We discovered it was quite a great city. Like most Indians, Viney was familiar with the story regarding the 1893 World Parliament of Religions held in Chicago one year after the World's Fair that celebrated the 400th anniversary of Columbus' first voyage to the New World. Swami Vivekananda represented India and Hinduism at the Parliament. This was the reason Viney's father regretted not going to Chicago.

Swami Vivekananda spoke several times during the course of the meetings, receiving a two-minute ovation in response to the first words he spoke: "Sisters and brothers of America!" He talked about differences among religion, the significance of Buddhism, the need for missionaries to help the poor in India before trying to save their souls, and most famously introducing the United States and the representatives of many countries to Hinduism. Swami Vivekananda was a sensation in the U.S. His speech on Hinduism was printed in newspapers across the country. He was the first truly famous Indian of modern times in the West and as a result became famous in India. That legacy remains in India, the moment that India was on the world stage for the first time. Viney felt a spiritual bond with Chicago as a result. And we felt much better about taking this leap of faith on our odyssey.

Before moving to Canada, we already knew that there was a big difference between living somewhere and just visiting, even if the visit is a long one. After our postings around India and our experiences as expats in Iraq and Saudi Arabia, we were prepared to adapt to a new culture while retaining our Indian identity. But immigrating is far different from working as an expat. Expats are given good salaries and often many benefits, like a car or house to use. Immigrants are starting fresh, almost like a young adult who needs a job, maybe additional education, and must be careful about money.

All in all, our immigration to Canada was perhaps the best thing that had happened in our lives after our experiences in the Middle East. Our Canadian experience not only uplifted our own family, but also gave us a distinct status in India among our extended family members. They all now had an opportunity and reason to visit North America. They could learn whether immigrating to or studying in Canada suited them. To some extent, we have done much of the research for them. We learned many new lessons as a result of our move to Toronto with the intention of becoming Canadian nationals. Those lessons can be very helpful to would-be Canadians.

- *Be mentally prepared that your foreign qualifications and experience are not recognized.* Every employer wanted us to have local experience, but how could we if every employer had that criterion for hiring? Eventually, we found employers willing to let us gain local experience. We had to accept entry level jobs, though, positions similar to the ones we had fifteen years before when we completed our master's degrees. And those master's degrees were just pieces of paper to Canadian employers. Promotion required us to essentially repeat our graduate courses or take courses in new skills important to the employer.
- *Set aside ego.* In a new culture, particularly one radically different from what one has known, one must accept that gaining knowledge of the local culture is going to take effort and a lot of time. Accept the fact that you will embarrass yourself or at least feel ashamed, even when everyone else recognizes you just didn't know. Watch how locals act in various situations and locations.
- *Never assume a word you recognize is being used the way you use it.* No matter how skilled you may be with the local language, local vocabulary differs in almost every tongue. We had been using English almost as much as Hindi for years. How were we supposed to know that a "donut" is a breakfast food and a car tire? They are both toroid (circular tubes with a hole in the middle). Even if you look "donut" up in most dictionaries, it will just say the word is a variant of "doughnut."
- *Live modestly in the beginning.* As landed immigrants, we had no limit to baggage we could bring, but most of our things were shipped, including all of those Persian carpets still with us today. We found that garage sale items are fine. So are thrift shops. Commuting by bus or subway is generally a pleasant way to travel anywhere that public transportation is good. Even though we were cautious about buying a car, we discovered that auto insurance for new residents is scandalous. Coverage for an old car can cost $2000-$3000 per year. After one begins to get experience driving in Canada, the rate goes down gradually. The whole point of living modestly is this allows one to save to

buy your own apartment or home. Property ownership brings new sorts of bills, but Canada also offers tax credits, and it improves one's credit history. Best of all, you gain a unique sense of ownership, and any children you have will be thrilled by the chance to have separate rooms.

- *Prepare for different climates.* Most of India has two seasons more or less, although mountainous areas can become quite cold in winter. The Middle East seems to have one season. Canada's winters are extremely cold, and all immigrants need to be as much mentally prepared as materially prepared with coats, gloves, hats, and mufflers. Surviving winter in Canada is easier in some ways than the milder winters in India. Most Indian homes don't have air conditioning or heaters. Inside is the same as outside. In Canada, one can get comfortable and cozy at home despite the chill outside.

- *The quality of life depends on how much freedom exists and how taxes are used.* Canada is justly proud of providing liberty and freedom for everything: expression, business, employment, education, religion, speech, etc. The only restrictions are laws that prevent one person from infringing someone else or prohibit discrimination. Freedom of movement means no one cares where you go or what you do. Quality of life offers a very positive experience. It isn't just that Canadians don't throw garbage in the streets, as is common in India, or hygiene habits are more advanced. That quality of life also includes many reassuring benefits that come at the price of taxes. We paid no taxes in the Middle East since we lived in oil-rich countries but lacked the basic freedoms so critical for human growth. Now we had 40 percent deducted from our gross pay. However, in exchange the Canadian welfare system provided excellent, free medical facilities and outstanding education that included making sure students learned French, given the large Francophone population in the country. We even received an allowance for our kids, C$33 a month for each child at the time. Above all, we enjoyed complete freedom. That was priceless.

- *Negative effects and events will come from unexpected sources.* Junk food seemed especially helpful when parents are so busy with work and have no time. However, kids become addicted. Varun was drinking Coke daily and started gaining weight. It took a lot of effort, including starting exercise, to shed the weight over some years. The whole experience with the used car dealer and obtaining a judgment that was useless baffled us. And we were exposed to drug-related crimes for the first time. Having tenants in our basement was fine with the right tenants. However, at one point we rented to two young males who acted as though they had been spoiled growing up. They stayed up late drinking and playing loud music or went out drinking and brought girls back with them. Then they started drinking on the curb in front of our house. We were particularly concerned for our daughter. She was in grade eight and alone in the house for an hour or so after school. We had to call the police a few times due to their behavior. Canada tries to be fair to everyone, and tenants have rights just as landlords do. With a lot of effort and intervention by their mothers, we managed to send them off. We were slowly but surely learning the ways of life in a free society.

- *A culture created from immigrants provides far greater rewards than one based on a people who have inhabited a place for centuries.* Aside from the First Nations, who were actually immigrants many millennia ago, Canada is an immigrant society. Some European countries have contributed large numbers, such as England, Scotland, Ireland, France, Italy, and Germany. However, the country has become even more multicultural, with easy opportunities to make cross-cultural friends as a result of landed immigrants coming from Asia, Eastern Europe, and the Arab world. Other countries, like Great Britain, France, Brazil, Argentina, and Chile, are nations of immigrants, too. However, they tend to only attract people who have ties to them. Canada, like the U.S., is an immigrant country with people from all over the world. Especially in Toronto, finding a new appreciation for cultural differences is only a matter of exploring various neighborhoods and suburbs to discover restaurants serving the wide variety of cuisines available. We have encountered some discrimination due to being brown-skinned Indians, but on the whole no one really thinks they are superior, as the French did on our visit to Paris

MBA – University of Toronto
1994

Toronto 1994

Saudi heat was a thing of the past
In Canada. Kids learn hard lessons of immigration

Viney's first employer in Toronto
1990-94

Toronto 1994 –
Hurray! We are Canadians

1993 - Niagara Falls
Father enjoying the
Beauty of the falls

Five brothers at the time of father's
Sudden death in 1996.
Gobindgarh, India

United States (1994-97)

"Our battered suitcases were piled on the sidewalk again; we had longer ways to go. But no matter, the road is life."
Jack Kerouac

Lady luck was smiling. Everything fell into place in Canada in time for our move to the United States of America.

- Went to oath-taking ceremony becoming Canadian citizens and had our new passports issued in June 1994.
- Viney's second MBA from the University of Toronto was finished in May 1994, and the convocation awarding the degree was held in June 1994.
- Tenneco Automotive, the parent company, offered Viney a compelling opportunity to move to the head office in Chicago in June 1994 and advance upward to become Global Director of Quality. Viney accepted the offer.

Who could imagine how far Viney would reach in such a short time? He had started with the job of Junior Payroll and HR Clerk. Four years later, he became Global Director of Quality, with a worldwide span of control reporting to Luan Watkins, Global Vice President of Quality. Viney had access to the CEO of a five billion dollar company on a regular basis. Not only was Viney given a fresh opportunity to expand his horizons, the whole family did as well. Kumud had a chance to write a new chapter in her career. Megha and Varun had a chance to excel and discover new avenues for higher education and careers.

Viney's office leadership team in Toronto gave him a memorable farewell dinner, sending a limo to his home to go to dinner at the restaurant high in CN Tower. They truly were going to miss him as part of the team. Aside from the union formation in the company where Viney was blindsided, everything had gone smoothly under his watch. Even all of the staff and workers signed a big plaque as a farewell card. With that, we were set to move to the U.S. Viney

106

received an L-1 visa as an employee being transferred within the company, and the other three members of the family received L-2 dependent visas, only good as long as Viney had his L-1, but the L-2 dependent visa allows family members to work.

International moves handled by a large company amaze us. They are quick, thorough, and gracious, giving one hardly anything to worry about. Perhaps some global firms are stingier, but Tenneco Automotive took care of aspects of the move we would not have considered. While we knew the company was paying to move our household goods, we were surprised that the movers boxed everything carefully packed and labeled. Then they dropped them off in the correct rooms and opened them to make it easier for us to unpack.

The corporation gave us a real estate agent, rental car and home for two months, plus scouted for schools. They moved our cars. They paid the difference in our home sale price and the price we bought the house originally in Canada. They helped financially to buy our new home in Illinois. They filed for our green cards within six months of arrival. Nothing but extraordinary care for a smooth transfer was the overarching rule. It was perhaps the best move of our life, with everything falling in place so well.

We found a beautiful four bedroom house in Gurnee, Illinois, on the northern outskirts of Chicago. The house was bigger and less expensive than our house in Canada. Viney's commute time remained only a 15-minute drive. Gurnee itself was an up-and-coming community with plenty of stores and a discount mall. Our children got settled in their new schools quickly. Fortunately, they were transferring at the start of a new school year. A school bus picked them up and dropped them off right outside our home.

Varun was in fourth grade by then. He typically didn't say much, so we weren't surprised that he never said anything about missing his Canadian friends. Megha started tenth grade, high school. She kept in touch with Canadian friends. In addition to the normal curriculum, her focuses were on French immersion courses and playing soccer. The French helped when Viney's former boss sent his son for four weeks to live with us to improve his English. Having had to adapt so many times to new cultures and rules ourselves, we weren't the least bit shocked that our Parisian teenage guest did not realize he could shower anytime he wanted.

As we mentioned, Tenneco moved for Viney's green card within six months of our arrival in the U.S. The company paid the substantial fees for the lawyer and everything else involved in obtaining a green card. The application was approved early in 1996, after about a year. Now the whole family had green cards establishing permanent residency in the U.S. That meant we had the option of staying in the U.S. or going back to Canada after Viney's current assignment was over.

Kumud found employment as a sales associate at Kohl's, a departmental store. Fortunately, expats with L-2 visas can work immediately. After a short stint with Kohl's, Kumud decided to move on to a new profession: teaching. While her jobs in Canada and India were with banks, she discovered the pay for bank employees is much lower in the U.S. comparatively, and it takes much longer to get promoted. In 1995, Kumud successfully applied to become a substitute teacher in the middle school Varun attended. This arrangement gave Kumud enough time to spend establishing our new home but also many opportunities to be called in to work. On those days, she could even drive Varun to school. Finding so much enjoyment from this, Kumud started improving her educational qualifications through courses at nearby Lake County College.

Viney's settlement in his new office went extremely well. The office staff members were welcoming. He was well recognized as a key member of the global leadership team. He acquired yet another wonderful supervisor in Luan Watkins. Having a very rich global profile in his job, Viney visited many U.S., European, and Latin American units with his boss. Naturally, they got to know and respect each other quite well and became good friends. We still stay in contact with her and the family.

For the first time, Viney saw how U.S. companies functioned internally, the impact of networking, and the global dimensions, including European and Asian exposure. He had before him an opportunity to benefit the company while demonstrating his talents and experience. Under his leadership, most of the company units globally received ISO 9001 certification - 61 units out of 73. This great feat was accomplished in a short, two-year period.

Tenneco decided Viney was an up and coming leader who had greater leadership potential. The company sponsored his enrollment in one of Northwestern University's prestigious Kellogg Executive Leadership Programs, called the Executive Development Residential Program in Evanston, near Chicago. This was like doing another MBA but concentrated into a mere three weeks, unlike the two traditional MBAs Viney had completed in India and Canada.

By 1996, Viney was fully established in his head office job and was recognized as a potential leader, someone who could still succeed with even more responsibility. In the midst of the positive condition of our lives, on September 30, 1996, Viney's father died suddenly due to a stroke. Naturally, his passing was a big blow to our family and Viney's brothers' families. Viney's father had been running his own 10+2 school in Mandi Gobindgarh, Punjab. The school gets its name from adding the traditionally college-level grades 11 and 12 to grades 1 through 10. His school enrolled 1,200 children. No one in the family was prepared to take over his mantle. Viney's family attempted to manage the school leadership with the help of outside principals to fill the great gap that had been left. Ultimately, they had to sell the school in 2001. They felt a new sense of grief parting with their father's legacy.

Viney's father was an iconic figure, and his personality was based on strict principles. Each one of his sons not only inherited genes from him, they also acquired some part of his personality. He was an educator, orator, politician, singer, and, above all, a hard core zealot for Indian values. That constancy in embracing India as more than just land and instilling India as a philosophical, diverse culture permeated his being. He wanted his sons to find that same identity, and most of his sons did. Viney and his brothers all have some of their father in their personalities. Indeed, these qualities are so transparent, the wives of these men comment when they see their husbands acting like their father.

At the time of his death, we had fresh, vivid memories of Viney's father's stay with us. His Canada and U.S. visit from May to June in 1993 was a life-changing experience for him. Viney's father loved the society he encountered and even expressed a desire to immigrate to Canada. Had he lived a few more years, this desire could have been fulfilled with ease. He looked forward to a second opportunity to enjoy Canada and the U.S. and had been planning to return. He thought he might sell his school and immigrate.

During the two and a half years from our move in 1994 to the beginning of 1997, the time before and after this sad event, Viney visited most of the company units in the U.S., Europe, Latin America, and Asia-Pacific, a rare feat that even the top leaders of the company, including the CEO, had not done. At one point, he was offered classes to reduce his Indian accent. However, Viney thought that a global company should have people with all kinds of accents when speaking English. Looking back, Viney can see that it would have been a good idea to take the classes. In the 1990s, brown skin and accented English in the business world excluded one from "the club." Fortunately, Tenneco only wanted him to communicate more smoothly because he was rising in the company. Clearly, nothing about him was any kind of impediment to promotion.

We cannot describe this part of our odyssey any way other than to say we underwent a pleasant, smooth transition that was very healthy for the entire family. In the beginning, we did not fully realize how many opportunities could come our way. Then, in the beginning of 1997, Viney was offered a new role within the company, a more responsible regional leadership job. His supervisor, Luan Watkins, left Tenneco. In fact, she left the whole world of corporate business to start an antique store. For us, this step for her opened our eyes to the fact that people can leave their comfort zone to pursue their passion. We didn't realize at the time how soon we would be following her example. The new position offered to Viney, however, seemed more like returning to a comfort zone because the spot required moving to Delhi. However, before we move our story halfway around the world, we should discuss the impact on us of living in the U.S.

Slowly, we had become a part of U.S culture. In the years in Illinois before and after our stay in India, we took vacations every year. Viney travelled so much for work and could never fully forget work. However, we knew the U.S. offers so much variety, maybe even greater than India. Vacations were opportunities to share experiences as a family. We explored places near the four corners of the continental U.S.: Boston in the northeast, Seattle in the northwest, Los Angeles in the southwest, and Miami in the southeast. Who can ever forget one's first visit to Disneyland?

On the other hand, some travel experiences are best forgotten. Unfortunately, it seems that we will never forget our family drive from Chicago to Orlando and Miami and back to Chicago. As usual, we had rented a car for the trip to enjoy the comforts and reliability of a new car. We decided upon leaving Miami that if we could drive all of the way back with no significant breaks, we could save the price of one day on the rental car. We started off from Miami at 10 p.m. After driving continuously, we reached Chicago at 8:00 p.m. the following day, a mere 22 hours after we left southern Florida. Viney drove most of the way. Kumud had to quickly react to a sofa in the highway near Atlanta that could have caused a serious accident. All in all, deciding to rush back with only one principal driver to cover that distance was a major tactical blunder. Never again.

Despite making full use of the opportunities that came our way to learn, several aspects of American culture have been much more confusing than others. For example, in India sports are not a profession; they are a hobby that primarily focuses on soccer. Only cricketers make good money. In the U.S., people are fanatical (hence the word fan) about different sports and different professional teams. Teams earn huge sums from ticket, advertising, and broadcast sales. They use all of that money not to build places for their teams to play, but to bid for the best and most popular players, and to line the owners' pockets. Some players attract huge endorsement deals. Those deals can earn athletes much more than winning tournaments in tennis or races in skiing. Even the U.S. Olympic Committee searches for sponsors so they can pour funds into athlete training. Becoming a professional athlete requires hard work, talent, and luck. It isn't surprising to see why so many Americans try so hard to make it, dreaming of breaking into the elite ranks.

As seasons have expanded, there are no breaks in the calendar. NHL ice hockey and NBA basketball start in autumn and go through winter to playoffs in the spring. They begin in the middle of the NFL football season that runs from August to January. Major League Baseball holds "spring" training in February and March, then plays through spring and summer until the World Series concludes after the NHL and NBA have started their seasons. In the end of October and beginning of November, all four major sports are in action. No other country that we know has anything like the role of professional sports in U.S. culture. The U.S. is also unique in being about the only country other than Vatican City and North Korea where sports fanaticism does not focus almost exclusively on the original game of football: soccer.

Another aspect of entertainment where the U.S. differs is the movies. Hollywood is shorthand for all U.S. filmmaking, although independent production companies have become a larger part of the industry. The stars of Hollywood movies make millions. Female stars complain, justifiably, that they are paid less than their male co-stars. However, billions of women in the world could probably swallow any feelings of sexism to make $6 million versus $11 million for a few months' work. And compare that to the most anticipated Hindi movie for 2015, *Wazir*, made for less than $5 million. That's less than the salary for a female star. In fact, U.S. films made for less than $5 million is one definition of an independent production.

Just as Hollywood means movies to much of the world, Bollywood means movies in India. Bollywood films are world famous and popular in scores of countries. The ideas and plots are often copied from foreign films, but no one minds as long as it's entertaining. We were so surprised how big they are in Turkey, Iraq, Saudi Arabia, and Afghanistan. The actors' compensation in India is far below their colleagues' in the U.S. However, ticket prices are much lower and Bollywood movies tend to stay in theaters for a very long time, gradually earning money. There is a changing trend now in Bollywood, though, where the first couple of weeks determine any movie's success. American movie tickets cost at least $10. Movies are pulled from theaters in less than two months, shorter if they bomb, never getting the opportunity to build an audience. A major U.S. picture that does not rank number one on its release weekend or does rank first but earns less than expected is a failure. Those first weekend earnings of that "failure" could be the amount two Bollywood films make in months' long runs.

As with entertainment, we also find more serious socio-cultural issues take interesting turns as a result of our "foreign" perspective. For example, in the debates about marriage equality, opponents argued that same-sex marriage would destroy traditional marriage. That is really an unprovable claim, since no one could know the effect of same-sex marriages on male-female marriages unless same-sex marriages are allowed. But there is something missing from the argument. For years, everyone has accepted that around 50 percent of marriages in the United States end up in divorce. A part of this figure may be explained by states loosening the grounds for divorce. However, this high rate was reached after it was acceptable for couples to live together first. What have these people been finding out about their spouses or relationships in marriage that they didn't already know?

Our decision to marry broke with the tradition of arranged marriage. However, we hadn't known each other for long when Viney proposed. More than half of all marriages in India are still arranged by the couples' families. Most expat Indians still go back and choose a spouse in a matter of weeks. Marriages tend to last because it is a marriage between two families, it is a sacrament rather than a contract, and divorce is very shameful, especially for women. One of the strengths of arranged marriages is that families look for candidates who match the economic, social, and educational background of their marriageable offspring. In other words, the prospective husband and wife share many attributes and are therefore likely to be compatible. For decades, India's divorce rate has been around one percent, considered the lowest among any country providing these statistics.

Since the 1970s, more and more women in India have found employment outside the home. More and more women have entered professional fields. When both partners have responsible, secure positions and strong, rational opinions, it is much easier during a dispute not to give in than to find a compromise. India's divorce rate has increased in the last decade while this phenomenon of women entering professions has been going on. If the couple has children, they are more likely try to find a middle ground that avoids divorce and resolves the worst issues. But if they have no children and both have decent incomes, the worst problems in the aftermath of divorce don't exist.

The BBC had a headline in 2011 that the divorce rate in India had risen 100 percent, and the government was quite concerned. Of course, an increase of 100 percent in one percent means the divorce rate rose to two percent. By all reports, the rate still remains below five percent, and the increases have been almost exclusively in urban areas among middle and upper class couples. Rural areas, where arranged marriages remain the norm, have seen no measurable increase in divorces. One possible reason is that nuclear families consisting of a couple and maybe children have become more prominent in urban areas, while the traditional multi-generational joint family that reinforces the family unit is still practiced in villages and small towns.

India and the United States retain that urban-rural divide in a variety of ways. Nonetheless, the differences between cities and countryside are far greater in India. For as large as the United States is, in many ways it is not as diverse as India. Although it was formed from states that considered themselves politically distinct, the only real cultural differences were the slave-owning economy in the South and pockets of non-British immigrants like the Dutch along the Hudson River and the Swedes in Delaware. New states were formed primarily by people moving west from the original thirteen, carrying their culture with them. Differences arose due to geography, economics, and isolation until telecommunications became widespread. With movies, television, and the Internet, American culture, at least in terms of entertainment, has become homogenous. Even the growing political divisiveness is just one perspective looking at its opposite rather than any real sign of diversity.

India, on the other hand, was formed from a jigsaw puzzle of independent kingdoms and principalities, remnants of the Mughal Empire, and cities built by Europeans. Even as Britain's "Jewel in the Crown", the territory that is now India was never governed as a whole entity until independence. The people and cultures still vary greatly. So, though it may seem like oversimplification or stereotyping to draw general lessons from our experiences in the

114

United States, our observations have been varied enough to have taught us a few things.

- *With the right education, the sky is the limit for professional and personal growth.* The availability of opportunities rises and falls depending on the overall economy and the financial health of your employer. Education plays a huge role in how well one can take advantage of these opportunities. Certainly, other factors like work habits, personality, and ability play their part. However, as we discovered by Viney taking the Kellogg Executive Development Program and Kumud taking education courses at Lake County College, further education adds to one's profile and never goes to waste. And taking classes is not the only way to become better educated. Community service is much more prevalent in the U.S. than anywhere else. Raising money, working with sports teams, or volunteering in other ways feeds personal growth. The experiences give you a chance to learn in a different environment and support you in achieving the higher levels of Maslow's hierarchy theory on personal development. The lessons translate into improving your work.
- *From an outsider's perspective, the United States is a free society in every respect.* The limitations we have seen on freedom arise from individual action and perception. For example, most Americans either don't take the vacation time allotted to them by their employers or they stay connected to work one way or the other while away. Another example is marriage. At first glance, two people meeting, learning about each other, perhaps living together, and loving each other sounds like a firm foundation for a lasting union. In reality, that freedom to choose a spouse unites two individuals who can easily find grounds for separating. Offspring in India have much less control over whom they will marry, but the choice is made between two families that see marital union as the initial bond in a long lasting alliance.
- *Equality is a spectrum, not an absolute.* India is relatively backwards when it comes to how women are treated socially and legally compared to men. However, some communities are

matriarchal. There was little opposition to Indira Gandhi becoming prime minister in 1966 near the height of the feminist movement in the U.S. And her daughter-in-law, Sonia Gandhi, has been president of the Indian Congress Party since 1998. Meanwhile, the major U.S. parties have nominated just two women as vice presidential candidates, and no female presidential candidates ever. The Middle East is worse than India. Iraq restricted women to certain roles. However, Saudi Arabia wins the "top prize", as it were; the Kingdom is known throughout the world for imposing substantial restrictions on women, even prohibiting them from driving. Despite lapses like having only two women running for president out of an initial field of twenty-three for the 2016 U.S. election, Western countries are light years ahead in equality between the sexes compared to the Middle East and South Asia.

- *Globalization is eliminating ethnic and racial discrimination in the business world.* Discrete discrimination in the form of not getting a promotion still can occur. When Viney's supervisor asked him to take classes to improve his accent, the intent was only to help him get along better in the U.S.; there was no indication that having an accent was hindering his promotion. Viney refused at the time because his accent was part of his identity as a global citizen. Now Viney knows that global citizenship comes from what one experiences and learns, not from sounding different in a second language, and regrets not having taken the class.

- *Innovation has been and remains the key to the U.S. economy's strength.* So many cutting edge ideas and products have come from the United States in the last 150 years or so. The U.S. is fortunate to have the resources, creative climate, and varied market that something new is always being introduced. In Singapore, Viney went to a cardiologist who had studied in the U.S. His view on the innovation mentality was interesting. Singapore is a small city-state without the resources to innovate. However, it is wealthy enough from being a business hub that hospitals and companies have the ability to acquire innovations from the U.S. Quality innovations keep the U.S. a leader in the global economy. Not all of these innovations have had a positive impact. The U.S. created fast food, junk food, and frozen and canned food, all laden with sodium, fat, and poor carbohydrates. As we learned from Varun's chubby period, it is far too easy to get caught up in the convenience and temporary pleasures these products offer.

- *Stay visible, raise your hand, and make sure people can recognize you.* Oftentimes, people do not take advantage of raising their hands to get opportunities. In 1992, when Viney was the human resources manager, his boss wanted someone to lead the ISO 9001 project. To insure the work was objective, he wanted someone who was outside the quality control structure. He also needed someone who could lead a team effectively. Viney volunteered based on the skills he had that were vital to the success of the project. He got the job done in his unit, and that led to his promotion and our move to the U.S. Viney was there, volunteered, and performed the task. Employees that remain in the shadows, never raise their hands, and have little to show when asked to demonstrate their performance can hide for a while, but they will eventually be found and dismissed. Another way of looking at this is to see your professional progress as a growing tree. If the tree tries to just grow a trunk and rise vertically, it can't get very far. Tree trunks rarely have leaves, without leaves the tree can't convert sunlight into food, and without food the tree will die. Instead, trees grow branches reaching out horizontally, and the branches grow leaves. The leaves photosynthesize food from sunlight. The food makes the trunk rise higher and provides the energy to make more branches with more leaves. One's goal professionally needs to be acting like a branching tree, looking horizontally to find opportunities to learn side roles and broaden your knowledge of the company or business.

- *Unity and diversity are just opposites of the same coin.* The United States is one unit, but it is also some 57 units if one looks at the states, District of Columbia, Puerto Rico, Guam, and other territories. Hardly anyone immigrates to India, yet communal diversity and regional histories challenge unity. Almost everyone in the U.S., except the American Indian nations, has immigrated from elsewhere or is descended from someone who did. A lot of people arrived recently. In 2013, the government said that 13 percent of the U.S. population was made up of immigrants and 12 percent was a first-generation American. However, most immigrants settle in large cities, leaving huge areas where residents do not encounter this diversity. Those people get the false impression that the U.S. is more homogeneous than it actually is. Working for a large global company, one meets people from all over, and one goes all over. Suddenly, you realize that "It's a Small World", introduced at the 1964 World's Fair in New York City, was an accurate prediction.

India (1997-98)

"The whole object of travel is not to set foot on foreign land;
it is at last to set foot on one's own country as a foreign land."
G. K. Chesterton

After Luan Watkins left Tenneco at the end of 1996, Viney's new boss came just at the start of a reorganization of the company. As part of the changes, Viney was asked to become the new Asia Pacific Director of Manufacturing and Quality based in Delhi. This was a great opportunity. It was a dream come true to go back to India, our motherland, as U.S. residents and Canadian citizens; we were going to be expatriates in our home country within 15 years of originally leaving our home country. Indeed, whatever country issued our passports had become irrelevant because we had become global citizens, expats wherever we lived from now on.

As much as it seemed like a terrific offer, extensive discussions within the family for this move were necessary. It was a little scary for us to think of uprooting ourselves once again after another short stint somewhere. But we had been seizing chances and taking risks for two decades. Kumud was angry about continuing this pattern of moving that had started with Viney's posting to Hyderabad, Shillong and Simla. However, she also knew the culture of the proposed destination, unlike everywhere else where we had relocated to. We would sit at the kitchen table and list the pros and cons, just as we always did for all major decisions. The review always ended in a draw. We finally decided sometime at the end of June or beginning of July 1997 to take the assignment and move to India.

Megha was in her senior year in high school, so whatever we decided, she was heading for college and would not be living with us. We dropped her off at college in Omaha. She entered the pre-med program at Creighton University, a Jesuit school. The program guaranteed admission to medical school with a high GPA. We never knew if she wanted to be a medical doctor, but at that point that seemed to be her intention, as well as our own. Now here she was fulfilling her grandfather's desire for Viney to become a doctor. Megha knew she would have no home to go to during breaks, although she would be able to visit us in Delhi over the summer. Of course, leaving our daughter by herself was heart-wrenching for Kumud, more so because we would be so much farther away than if we were staying in Chicago. We settled her in her dormitory. At the end of August 1997, we said goodbye and good luck to Megha with heavy hearts and headed for Delhi soon thereafter.

Although our ability to remember events and people is quite good, sometimes we have some difficulty remembering the date something happened. We vividly recall that at the end of August 1997, just as we were moving to India, Diana Princess of Wales died so unexpectedly. Within a week, Mother Teresa also died. Both of them were favorite role models for Kumud. She already felt burdened moving to Delhi. Those public tragedies and leaving our daughter in her dormitory in a strange city put her in an even more somber mood and taxed her greatly.

The logistics of the transfer were not really difficult. As an expat, the company took care of everything in India, including a car with a driver, accommodations, round-trip airfare for our daughter to visit us once a year, and a live-in maid who was a tremendous help to Kumud. We really had no choice about schools for Varun. In order for him to continue with an American curriculum, the only option was the American Embassy's school in Delhi. This worked out well because he was able to go on school trips to places like Rishikesh and Haridwar, the self-titled Yoga Capitals of the World and Gateways to the Himalayas, where Varun went canoeing on the Ganges. Exploring India was a great treat for Varun since he had never lived in his parents' homeland.

The first break in an American university's schedule is for Thanksgiving. Since Megha couldn't make the trip to Delhi for such a short period, she went to Boston to spend time with close family friends of ours. During that week, we received a horrifying call from some of Megha's friends that her college roommate had committed suicide. Being there for our daughter was difficult given the distance. We tried desperately to reach Megha in Boston before she learned this tragic news. We decided to arrange for a friend to fly to Omaha to be with her for the week after the break. This sad event burdened Kumud further, both out of sympathy for the roommate's parents and anxiety about Megha's emotional well-being.

Naturally, Kumud's concerns about being in India grew. We knew we were supposed to stay for three years. Kumud understood that Viney would have to travel all over East Asia, as well as to Singapore, Australia, and New Zealand, and more for his job. In fact, eighty percent of the time Viney was travelling. Even though Kumud was in a familiar environment and her mother was living with us, she could not reverse the day-by-day deterioration in her health. Proximity to family still only provided for sporadic visits and little comfort.

Viney made every effort to ameliorate the situation. Kumud and Varun travelled with Viney to Bangalore and Chennai a few times. Kumud even visited Viney in Singapore while he was there on business. It was our first exposure to this beautiful city-state. We were so swept up by its vibrancy and modernity, we vowed to return some day to live.

All of the worries and concerns were taking a heavy toll on Kumud. We contemplated moving to Singapore or Sydney. Unfortunately, we could not work out the logistics. Everything was so bad, we chucked the three-year assignment and decided we would move back to Chicago after only one year in Delhi. Viney expressed our desire to go back, and the arrangements were made for us to return to Chicago toward the end of 1998.

Global businesses routinely deal with having to move and reassign expat employees. They don't necessarily have a truly suitable position for the person transferring back from an expat assignment. However, if the expat is a valuable leader, the company will just give him whatever job remotely relatable to his qualifications that happens to be open. In late 1998, businesses and governments of all sizes were scrambling to create and put into place systems that would help them avoid issues when January 1, 2000, rolled around, the infamous Y2K problem. Tenneco offered Viney a new role as their Y2K Global Lead, overseeing all of the efforts to put systems in place to avoid any Y2K troubles. Although it sounded a bit like Viney's former role supervising ISO 9001 certification of the company's units, the substance of the work involved was not compatible with Viney's qualifications. This being the only job they offered him, Viney decided to leave Tenneco.

Leaving a job is tricky and uncomfortable. However, Viney landed in Anderson Consulting, later renamed Accenture, where he prospered. Although becoming a partner after a while was welcomed, Viney found that the greatest benefit was working with so many young IT specialists fresh out of university. Their exuberance, enthusiasm, and engagement made Viney and everyone else feel young, too. The consulting environment turned out to be more satisfying than anything Viney had tried previously.

As we had learned long before, short visits to a place cannot replace extended stays, even if one travels somewhere that is very familiar. In 1997-98, we were seeing India through lenses crafted by our experiences living in Iraq, Saudi, Canada, and the U.S., and our exposure to so many cultures in our travels and interactions. We had the gift of being able to look at our native land with some detachment. That led to a few new insights.

- *The happy memories of a place make the negative aspects one encounters on return seem even more severe.* We knew that corruption in government and at every level of society was endemic in India. Since we had lived in North America, what we once meekly accepted as one of the "rules", we now sadly viewed as a weakness. The changes in India were visible and very positive. It was interesting to see how strong, reform-minded leadership could make a dramatic impact on the economy, culture and standard of living. Delhi's skyline had never been particularly clear, but the haze and air pollution ranked the city near the top of the list of the most polluted cities in the world. What a difference Toronto and even Chicago had been. Also, India is a hot country. The hottest season starts in February, peaks in May-June, and continues until September. The majority of our stay was during the extended summer. Facing any adversity is rendered more difficult if one is facing it in extreme weather conditions. What had been typical temperatures most of our lives became an added misery. But how important were any of these things? In retrospect, we wonder if it would have been better for the family to adjust for a couple of years and reap the economic benefits of expat status. Ten years earlier, we made it through living in Saudi Arabia. However, Kumud's health was paramount and becoming worse the longer we stayed. Our exit had to be much faster than we had planned.

- *Stability in leadership at the beginning of any project forms a rock-solid foundation for future progress.* India before 1981 was in many ways still struggling to find its footing. Our education and jobs gave us a view of how progress was being achieved, but progress was slow. Indian laws had been designed to protect industries from foreign competitors. Border wars with China and Pakistan showed there wasn't even agreement on what was and wasn't India. Since independence, rule by the Indian National Congress Party either with an outright majority or with allied parties had been the norm. This wasn't too unusual given the role Congress played in achieving independence. Japan's Liberal Democratic Party and Sweden's Social Democratic Party also ruled their countries continuously for decades.

- *A sound measure of the health of any institution is the ease of reaching compromise and avoiding conflict among diverse constituencies.* The continuity provided by Congress for half a century could not mask the tensions among communities. Two successive prime ministers had been assassinated in the 1980s, Indira Gandhi for her handling of Sikh calls for autonomy, and her son and successor Rajiv Gandhi for his handling of Tamil calls for autonomy. By 1996, Indians had become familiar with allegations of corruption resulting from power being held so long. The period of coalition governments began. On one side is a group of parties called the National Democratic Alliance (NDA) that emphasizes the good globalization has brought India. On the other side is the National Progressive Alliance (NPA), led by Congress, which calls for greater attention to the basic needs of poorer citizens. The NPA had a majority from 2004 to 2014, and the NDA ruled before and after. Although the coalitions contain likeminded national and regional parties, they aren't so likeminded that they can agree on a common legislative agenda without making policy compromises.

- *Opening a sealed chamber, such as a protectionist economy, creates a whirlwind.* On our return in 1997, much had changed, far more than we expected. The Congress government had instituted economic reforms after 1991, reforms that opened India to foreign investors and foreign goods. The impact of economic liberalization was visible regardless of where one looked or whom one saw. There was more prosperity. People of many levels saw their standard of living moving up. We could see U.S. fast food chains had sprung up everywhere, e.g. Domino's Pizza, Kentucky Fried Chicken, McDonald's, etc. Home delivery of groceries and meals had become commonplace. Multinationals flocked to India throughout the 1990s due to liberalization of the economy under reforms introduced by Narsimha Rao and Manmohan Singh. Suddenly, expats were moving to Delhi and other Indian cities. Property rental prices skyrocketed to meet the demand for housing that would be corporation-paid or occupied by someone with a substantial income for India. The four bedroom condo we moved into cost Rs160,000 per month, more than U.S.$4,000 per month. These prices were unbelievable in a country where average salaries were less than Rs5,000 per month.

Fourth Interlude:
Western Europe (1995-96 & 2003-09)

"Like all great travelers, I have seen more than I remember,
and remember more than I have seen."
Benjamin Disraeli

Viney visited Western Europe many times on business. Kumud accompanied him whenever possible. The region is similar to India in that there are many diverse communities that have a long history of conflict and cooperation. However, the various attempts to unify all or most of Western Europe, dating back to Charlemagne creating the Holy Roman Empire in 800, have, if anything, sharpened cultural divisions. The only unifying element for centuries was Catholicism, until the Reformation in the 1500s created a range of denominations. While India uses Hindi and English as languages that facilitate commerce and government, Europe stopped using Latin as a lingua franca in the 1600s, switching to French until the 1900s. However, these were languages used by elites and scholars. National languages and local dialects supported the survival of national and local customs and traditions. Even France until after World War II had significant populations that did not understand standard (Parisian) French. Now, the European Union has gone a long way toward unifying not only Western Europe, but most of the countries west of Russia. Even so, the EU counts 23 official languages, which keeps many translators busy and well-paid. Switzerland alone, not an EU member, has four official languages.

The diversity makes Western Europe an interesting place to visit. Every country, sometimes every city or district, has a distinctive cuisine and many famous architectural gems. Modern transportation networks make it easy to travel from one end to the other in a day at most. Our daughter was fortunate to be an exchange student in Switzerland during 2006-07. She completed one semester at a Swiss university in St. Gallen while completing her MBA studies at the University of Chicago. She had a wonderful experience studying there and traveling throughout Europe. Actually, we think she did more travel and less study due to the convenience of getting around. One time, Viney was in Milan for just a day and a half. Megha took the train just to have lunch with her father, returning to Switzerland the same day.

Opportunities to enjoy new experiences exist on every corner. Every visit makes one want to see more: cities we haven't seen yet, like Venice or Vienna, and all of Eastern Europe. The downside is that the traveler has to keep track of cultural differences like dining times, emphasis on punctuality, degree of formality toward business, and, despite the euro, currencies. After our visits to the UK and France in the mid-eighties, we now gradually became exposed to more lessons about the European way of life.

Viney first visited Germany in 1995 for Tenneco Automotive to discuss quality initiatives and tour automotive assembly plants. He had many subsequent visits under Accenture to Frankfurt, Munich, and Walldorf from 1999-2009. We were very impressed with the German way of life, especially the emphasis on structure, privacy, punctuality, thriftiness, and hard work. We had learned these same qualities early in our lives, and so we had a natural affinity for the German perspective. During our initial visits, the attitude of the Germans we met seemed neutral to unfriendly. At times, we felt they had a superiority complex. Language may have played a role in our perceptions; it seemed to be a barrier the first few times. Slowly, we got used to the situation and managed to find ways to communicate somehow.

The desire for orderliness that is part of the German stereotype permeates business life. We found in our office meetings that surprises and humor were not a norm. Jokes were considered odd and out of place. Everything seemed to be carefully planned out and decided upon, with changes rarely occurring after an agreement had been worked out. Even innovation had a structure to it.

Viney remembers:

I recall having stayed in Frankfurt at the Sheraton near the airport during my first visit in 1995. There were small bottles of liquor in the hotel room. I thought they are complimentary. I took all eight of them to Chicago, thinking the hotel had been so generous providing these gifts. I spent some time showing the little bottles to folks at

126

home and remarking how thoughtful Europeans are. When I got hit with a credit card charge of nearly $75 later on, I realized how wrong I had been. I had never considered that since hotels have a guest's credit card number, they could charge items even after we left the hotel. That was a good lesson for all our future visits. From then on, we expected charges for everything, even checking whether the bottled water was complimentary.

Spain, and Germany for that matter, is a country with widely varying regions. While we visited Madrid, Barcelona, and Bilbao over the course of many trips, we know Spain has much more variety to offer. Our initial impression of Spain was a country of bull fighting, *la siesta* after lunch, balancing work with pleasure, and creating an easy way of life. We were right on all counts. Business seems to revolve around meals and entertaining.

Lunch is the main meal every day, which accounts for the need for rest afterward before doing any work. Offices empty at noon for lunch and siesta and reopen at 3 p.m. Of course, we were not unfamiliar with this way of scheduling one's day. Saudi Arabians also rest after lunch when the day is hottest. We later found that the same happens in China. While we knew Spaniards preferred late dinners, we were surprised that this was practically enforced on everyone. Once we were in Madrid, looking to have an early business dinner around 8:00 p.m. To us, that seemed late. We could not find a single restaurant open in the center of the city until 9:30. Bars typically remain open until dawn. Once on an official visit, our group went out to a bar at midnight and stayed out until 5:00 a.m. The Spanish team members were fresh at 8 a.m. for our normal meeting, while we team members from the U.S. struggled to maintain some decorum and not fall asleep.

We visited Italy many times, also, although our trips were confined to Rome and Milan. We had heard a lot about Italy: home of the Roman Empire, birthplace of the Renaissance, creator of a rich cuisine featuring the best wines and cheeses, and headquarters to big fashion houses like Armani, Gucci, Versace, and Prada. We were very eager to see Italy and were not disappointed at all, even though the designers clearly were at the top of the high end and produced their unique clothes and accessories for export. Rome is best known for its wealth of historical structures, some of which are free to view. We had the chance to see the Colosseum, Pantheon, and the Trevi fountain. While we viewed St Peter's Basilica, we could not go to the Vatican City, so that must wait for a future visit.

Meetings are typically less formal than in Germany. Italians are known for their family-centric culture. There are numerous small and mid-sized businesses that are family-owned and operated. Even many of the larger companies, such as Fiat and Benetton, are still primarily controlled by single families. The dynamics in the familial structure can give way to a bit of chaos and animated exchanges in business settings.

Switzerland lies at the very heart of Europe, strategically located between the major European countries of Germany, France, and Italy, as well as Austria. As a result, this small country has three main languages—German, French, and Italian—plus the ancient Romansch dialect of Latin as its four official languages. Although English is not one of these languages, everyone we met understood it. The Swiss are a humble and law-abiding people. Unlike Italy and Spain, we were surprised to see the hosts of our meetings arriving before the scheduled time usually. We were told punctuality is expected, much as it is in Germany. However, the Swiss also relish festivals. Once we were in Zurich in February during Carnival. The celebrations were a sight to see, with street dancing, costumes, and parades.

We have always been interested in Scottish culture and are pleased to have had the opportunity to visit Edinburgh and Glasgow. We celebrated our twenty-fifth marriage anniversary in Edinburgh during the summer of 2004. The visit was our anniversary gift. It was a perfect place to rededicate ourselves for the next twenty-five years. The Scottish people have a genuine pride about their nationality and culture, and they know how to party. They are extremely friendly. We had great experiences interacting with them. Once, we got lost. A Scottish girl took special pains to get us a map and spent 10-15 minutes explaining not only the place we were to visit, but additional sites on the way. We were quite pleased that

Viney's niece in Toronto married an extremely nice Canadian gentleman of Scottish descent in 2015. Now the Kaushal family has an authentic Scottish flavor. The unique wedding ceremony took place aboard a cruise boat on Lake Ontario, with Indian and Scottish traditions observed. A bagpiper played beautiful music in the background, adding to the great experience for all.

Despite the differences among cultures, we observed certain similarities that provided us with new lessons.

- *Finding a pleasant balance between work and the rest of life is satisfying.* Life is short. Europeans enjoy life as fully as they can. A rich family culture is pervasive throughout all western European countries. Work is rarely as all-consuming as it is among North Americans. For example, Europeans do not mix vacation and work. While on vacation, they know how to unplug themselves and focus on relaxing with family. This is unlike most of us in North America who keep up with the office through cell phones and emails during vacation. In Germany and France, everyone goes on extended vacations in August, bringing business to a near halt.
- *European countries are less similar than other regions of the same size.* Each has its own rich heritage and cultural personality differences. They have different histories and different economies. Germans have a better, larger economy that sometimes makes them seem superior. France and the UK have close ties but engage in a constant rivalry. Spain and Italy have glorious pasts, but their economies now struggle. However, Europeans are similar in terms of their respect for freedom and human rights. Recent activities to bind the various countries closer, like the euro and the Schengen Treaty that allows unrestricted access to citizens of the member countries to the other countries, have been helpful and harmful. They improve economic ties, and Schengen increases the pool of candidates for jobs. But Greece created a lot of grief due to its economic problems that "Europe" had to resolve. Open borders give terrorists easier access. Europe is discovering that the pace of progress is often two steps forward and one step back.

129

Fifth Interlude: Nepal (1998)

*"To travel is to discover that
everyone is wrong about other countries."*
Aldous Huxley

We went to Kathmandu during the summer of 1998. It is the capital of and largest city in Nepal. Nepal is sandwiched between India and China and notable for having maintained its independence in colonial days and when its larger neighbors have squabbled over nearby territory. Nepal lays claim to being the only officially Hindu state in the world, although Buddhism is also practiced widely. Most of the nation's customs arise from Hindu and Buddhist traditions that have been adopted over centuries of exposure to the culture and traditions of both religions. Not surprisingly, since both religions are indigenous to India, many Nepali customs are similar to Indian customs. For example, like India, cows are sacred in Nepal. They go where they please. They sleep where they want. We saw them everywhere.

Even though Kathmandu lies in a large valley between four mountains, the city is 4,600 feet (1,400 meters) above sea level. By far the largest metropolitan area in Nepal, a stalwart of the city's economy is support for tourism. Every necessity for exploring the country's five climatic zones is available. The best known destination is the Himalayan foothills. Nepal is home to eight of the ten highest peaks on Earth. Unfortunately, we were not able to go to the Himalayan foothills and base camps due to health concerns. A less well known reason for visiting Nepal is gambling. Gambling in India is restricted to casino ships that sail far enough from the coast to be outside Indian legal jurisdiction. Indians go to Kathmandu to gamble the way Saudi Arabians go to Bahrain to drink alcohol.

We actually stayed in a casino hotel near the center of the city, not for the entertainment, but rather the location. We could walk to most places and shop. Like Turkey, bargaining in the markets is the norm. We were able to see many touristic places, and were very comfortable moving around. Among the sites were the Seto

Machhendranath Temple, sacred to Hindus and Buddhists; Maju Deval, a Shiva temple built in 1690 that offers great views and has become a popular meeting place; and Pashupatinath Temple, regarded as one of the most significant Hindu Temples of Shiva in the world, built sometime in the 17th century. We were rather shocked and scared when we came across the crematoria, the spots on the river where bodies are cremated quite openly. A more pleasant place was a hill overlooking the city, where we found the most excellent views of the sunset.

Our visit in 1998 was fortunately timed. Soon after, the country was plunged into more than a decade of turmoil that made it unsafe for tourists. Nepal was a monarchy headed by King Birendra. The king was widely respected. However, Maoist guerillas began a civil war in 1998 to abolish the monarchy. They were successful in the rural areas but never able to dislodge the army from towns and cities. In 2001, the king's son and heir allegedly murdered the king, queen, and seven other members of the royal family before committing suicide. The reason for the massacre has never been firmly established, but some thought Birendra's brother Gyanendra, who inherited the throne, may have been involved. Four years later, King Gyanendra took over all government control like a dictator to end the Maoist revolt. He was unsuccessful, but the Maoists called a ceasefire anyway.

Meanwhile, a democracy movement formed seeking representative government and an end to the monarchy. The huge numbers of poor in the urban areas supported democracy. The king agreed to hand sovereignty to the people in 2006, and the abolition of the monarchy took effect in 2008. The Maoists ended up winning the most seats in the assembly and formed a broad coalition government. However, one dispute after another kept toppling prime ministers and rearranging governing coalitions. The assembly never got around to writing a constitution. Elections in 2014 under a caretaker government led by the Chief Justice allowed the people to remove their support for the Maoists and other troublemakers, leaving two moderate parties with a majority. Disaster in the form of major earthquakes in the spring of 2015 brought worldwide attention to the country. Finally, in September 2015, Nepal's Constitution making it a federal, parliamentary state was proclaimed, and a month later a woman was nominated to become president.

Our visit to Kathmandu was too brief for us to fully explore the city or spend much time contemplating what we were able to see. However, in 2015, 17 years after our visit, we learned a most valuable lesson.

- *No one can fully appreciate events elsewhere unless they have been there.* The Nepal earthquake in April 2015 brought back memories of our 1998 visit. Nepal is by far one of the least developed countries we have visited. Our interest in seeing another state with a Hindu majority was tempered by the pain we felt seeing so much poverty. With its magnificent temples and access to the Himalayas, Kathmandu attracts numerous tourists and adventurers from all over the world. How many of them see the destitution and need? We will definitely go there again, and this time we would like to go to a Himalaya base camp. But any thought of returning brings back the emotional impact we felt when the earthquake happened. To truly see other people as people and not just figures in a photo or video, one must first journey to those people and see how and where they live.

United States (1998-2010)

*"Home is where the heart is, and my heart is
wherever I am at the moment."*
Lily Leung

After our initial move to the USA in 1994, we started a tradition
of writing a yearly letter to all our friends and family at Christmas
time. We know this once was fairly common. Americans began to
exploit opportunities wherever they might take them. Before long,
families were spread all across the country, and friends from school
were also dispersed. There had been no Internet with social media
sites for people to stay in touch with each other regularly. Since the
tradition of mailing Christmas cards was well established, it had
been a simple idea to include a Christmas letter with the card, one
or two pages describing what everyone in that household had done
that year. So in 1994, having now lived in five countries and traveled
to scores others, met people from all over, and had relatives and
friends in several countries, we started writing our own Christmas
letter. It had become too difficult to keep up with so many friends
and family, a total of about 150 individuals and families spread all
around the world.

The letter is a synopsis of key events during the year rolled into
one dense page. We have heard that Americans mostly stopped
sending Christmas letters because these missives were becoming
less welcome than fruitcake. Far too many of them went on far too
long about successes and achievements; they were becoming more
like opportunities to gloat rather than simply relaying news. We
seem to have avoided that charge. Despite the existence of
Facebook, Instagram, Twitter, blogging sites, and all to provide a
running commentary on one's "status" we have continued to inform
everyone about the highs and lows of the preceding twelve months
in a Christmas letter. Our friends are always eager to see the yearly
letter and start asking in November if we are preparing it. Actually,
we are somewhat proud to maintain a dying American custom,
knowing how important traditions are to cultural identity. We have

included some samples in the Appendix. Perhaps we can rekindle the idea in others of memorializing each year on paper for grandchildren and further descendants to learn who we were, just as we are doing with this book.

We mention the Christmas letter now, when our story shifts back to the U.S., because our return to Chicago became, thus far, the longest period we have lived in one place as a couple, and for Viney the longest he has lived anywhere. Although the annual letter began five years earlier, it is symbolic of a turn in our lives. The evidence was there with Kumud's reluctance to move to India and her illness that we knew had to be cured by first moving back to the U.S. Getting married is equated with settling down. That description was first applied most often to young men who had been sowing their wild oats. But in all cultures, marriage is a rite of passage associated with accepting new responsibilities and establishing a relationship and a home. We certainly spent time establishing a relationship and accepting new responsibilities, but given the number of times we had moved in twenty years of marriage, home was wherever our hearts were. With two children in tow, we had yet to settle down. Adopting the Christmas letter tradition was the first sign that our hearts wanted to stay in Chicago. The difficulties of our year in India made that clearer.

Returning to the U.S. was a great move for Kumud. Her health started improving slowly and steadily. We started construction of a new home, another positive contributor to Kumud's health. She was finally going to have a house she knew she could make into a home. We moved into that home at the start of 2001. That brought a sea change in Kumud's health and confidence. She began teaching high school full-time once again in 2002. In 2005, she bought a franchise for Club Z In Home Tutoring that she ran for three years. In this business, she hired teachers and sent them to the homes of students who needed private tutoring to do better in school. Kumud had grown from being a banker to an educator to an entrepreneur. While some of our journey's stops halted her development, Kumud still was able to broaden her knowledge and skill base and demonstrate her versatility. She did this while taking care of the housekeeping, holding down the fort wherever it was when Viney was away, and raising two children.

After moving into our home in 2001, we created another tradition from an idea that came during a solo meditation session. We decided to host a reunion once a year with six or seven close friends and their families spending one full week with everyone participating in planned activities. The first one was held at our house during Christmas week in 2001, definitively recognizing that we had established a physical home we wanted to share with others. The point, though, was to spend that precious commodity, time, with close, valued friends. Life is short. We always had taken risks to take full advantage of the years we have been given. Now, no risk was involved. Each year, we have planned a week in some location, created a schedule so everyone could share in all of the experiences, and went. After using Christmas week for a few years, we let the destination decide the time of year. So far, we have had these reunions in Chicago, Los Angeles, Seattle, Boston, Minneapolis, Whistler (British Columbia), Mexico, and Hawaii, as well as on cruises to Canada, the Caribbean, and Alaska.

Returning earlier from India than we had planned had left Viney in a vulnerable position with Tenneco. Companies do what they can to have positions available for expats at the end of their assigned time. Suddenly, the company needed to find something for Viney. In 1998, Y2K was a great source of anxiety in the business world and government. Everyone had information technology (IT) teams trying to identify what might happen to computer systems and create patches to fix any weaknesses. Tenneco offered Viney the lead job in the Y2K team. While Viney had demonstrated his ability as a manager who could complete projects, IT issues were not related to his field, and this was a stop gap position, and not a career enhancer. He refused the position and left Tenneco.

This was one of the boldest decisions Viney had ever made. He had such little time in the U.S. employment market. Kumud's health remained weak. However, leaving Tenneco turned out to be a blessing in disguise. His departure paved the way to join Anderson Consulting in 1999 (renamed as Accenture in 2001). Ironically, Accenture was and remains a unique IT consulting company. Viney was hired for an alliance management role, collaborating with about 160 other companies like Microsoft, Oracle, etc. His job was to oversee the coordination of projects with alliance partners that involved mutual clients. The partner companies gained income from the use of their products in the projects. Accenture gained from coordinating the implementation of new systems that clients needed to be more efficient in a rapidly globalizing environment.

Viney could not have imagined just how much experience he would obtain working to help create that globalizing environment for years to come. He enjoyed opportunities to work with many individuals visualizing the world as fully interconnected: theory leaders, CEOs, and accomplished professionals. These possibilities could not have arisen had Viney stayed working for an automotive parts firm. This was only possible in consulting companies like Accenture. To add to what was already an absolutely wonderful experience, Viney always felt young at heart while working because new hires were coming right out of university and MBA schools every year. Viney worked with them for 16 years in multiple roles, all with global portfolios that led him to tour the world many times until he finally retired in 2015.

While we were enjoying our personal and professional successes, our two children were entering adulthood. After finishing high school in 2002, Varun enrolled at the University of Waterloo in Waterloo, Ontario, a town west of Toronto. As a Canadian citizen, he thought that would get him off to a good start. After two years, he decided to return to Chicago. He transferred to the University of Illinois-Chicago, where he completed his BS in computer science in 2007. After graduating, he joined Accenture in Chicago as an IT consultant and had a fulfilling seven years serving many clients in the U.S. and abroad. Despite his career as a consultant, he managed to complete his master's of science in computer science from the University of Chicago. Currently, he is the IT lead in a mature start-up in Chicagoland that helps universities create and maintain online degree programs. Having gained an excellent education and a settled career, he is hoping to find a life partner. Given the amount of networking that goes on in the Indian community, we are helping to identify possibilities without arranging a match for him. That would be too ironic, given how we decided to marry. By virtue of his upbringing, he has turned out to be a global citizen with very broad perspectives of life.

After graduating with her bachelor's degree in 2001, Megha wanted a break year before diving into the rigors of medical school. She decided she wanted to do something different and applied for a position at Accenture. Being intelligent and diligent, Megha was offered a job and accepted. As the break year was ending, Megha realized she really enjoyed consulting and decided not to go to medical school. The old saying is that the wheel turns, meaning similar situations reappear in our lives at intervals. Ironically, Megha's decision was the same decision Viney had made years ago. She was paying her father back for what he did to her grandfather. However, this time she was following in her father's footsteps, not striking out on an entirely new path. With some initial disappointment, we now can see that she was never destined to become a medical doctor. She was fortunate to work for an employer who saw her talent and wanted to see her maximize her potential. After four years with Accenture, she decided to further her horizons with an MBA and was accepted at and attended the prestigious University of Chicago. Now, Megha is an accomplished executive with a global retail organization and lives in Boston.

Some memories stand out more vividly than others. Not surprisingly, they often involve a big step in your life or the life of a loved one. In 2006, Megha took the family out for Thanksgiving dinner. After dinner, she ordered tiramisu, one of the favorite desserts of the entire family.

She said, "I have something to share with you."

We were very curious but remained silent.

She continued, "This might be a surprise for you. I have a boyfriend."

That was certainly big news. Viney asked the obvious question. "Is he an Indian?"

Megha said, "Yes, he is from your motherland, but from southern India. His name is Vivek. You have met him once before in a group setting."

South India has a very different culture compared to Punjab, Delhi, and other parts of northern India. Traditionally, Indians from the north prefer to marry other Indians from the north. We had only met Indians from the south at work.

137

Megha and Vivek had met in Omaha of all places, at Creighton, where they were both pre-med students. We got to meet him formally a few months after she told us she was dating him. Our only concern was whether he was serious about the relationship. He said, "Yes, uncle and auntie, I am very serious." [He used the customary way younger Indians address all elders] However, then we learned he hadn't told his parents. Our feeling was that if he was truly serious, he ought to speak with his parents soon. He came from a distinguished Andhra family. He mentioned that his father was an orthopedic surgeon in the Cayman Islands and his mother was an educator like Kumud. Not much later, we received a call out of the blue from Vivek's parents. We told them we had no worries that they had chosen each other by themselves, just as we had done almost thirty years before.

Megha and Vivek married in 2009. Vivek is a medical researcher at Harvard. Their second son, Arvin, was born in November 2015 while we were writing this book. Vihaan, their first son, was born in May 2013. They are quite happy to have created their small family and recently moved into their own home in the Boston suburbs. Megha has the same international grooming and global perspective as Varun. We are truly blessed to have two very accomplished children and a great son-in-law who will continue our journey. All that seems missing is Varun's future life partner. We look forward to one day seeing the world through their eyes, and our grandkids' eyes.

Our most significant experience after returning to Chicago in 1998 was an internal journey. We had been religiously and spiritually inclined all through our lives. However, our formal orientation to spirituality started in 1999. Chinmaya Mission, a Hindu spiritual organization, was in the process of opening their North Chicago chapter in 1999 near our home. This is a value-based organization derived from ancient Hindu Vedanta philosophy teaching the richest values of life to create harmony and peace within one and with others and to uplift the human spirit. We took advantage of this new opportunity in our lives and joined as pioneer members of the chapter. With the efforts of like-minded professionals in the area who are also seekers of spirituality, the chapter was able to build a $3.5 million center on a seven acre parcel capable of hosting many daily and weekly activities, like weekend classes for children and adults to learn spiritual values. We became and remain very active in the organization, which has grown to include about 200 families with 450 children. While this provides an excellent opportunity to network with other like-minded people from India, our enthusiasm for Chinmaya Mission rests on the lessons from various ancient spiritual texts and other activities that have introduced us to and help us grow in spirituality. For example, adult classes teach understanding of scriptures, not just Hindu but also Sikh, Buddhist, and others. For the last sixteen years, our participation has brought a great balance to our lives.

We also have found many other activities that combine spirituality with philosophy, health, yoga, and meditation. These practices reinforce and provide deeper understanding of our spiritual being. They include:

- Yoga Camps with various Gurus and organizations
- Vipassana meditation sessions based on Buddhist philosophy
- Two week residencies in Bangalore, India, to participate in naturopathy retreats
- Art of living sessions
- Religious pilgrimages in India and other places around the world

The exposure through these dedicated efforts and committed time for spiritual and Yogic activities has given us a unique perspective on life, people, events, and above all the purpose of this mortal life. The final outcome for us is: one can only change oneself. That is the only control one has. One cannot directly change others. Only by changing oneself can one be a model of spiritual living that may attract others to seek to change themselves.

The whole family decided to make a special trip to India during December 2003 and January 2004. The first purpose was to visit all the places where we had lived in India and show our kids how past associations work. The second purpose was for us, after 25 years of wedded life, to marry each other once again with the same ceremony in front of our children.

To fulfill the first purpose, we visited Hyderabad, where Kumud came as a new bride. We went to the rice research institute where Viney had worked during 1977-79. We received a great welcome by the staff. They closed the institute for half a day to celebrate our return. This was a marvelous lesson for our children on just how precious old work relationships can be. We also visited Shillong, where we lived and worked from 1979 to 1981. The institute people prepared a gala reception for our family.

Although Megha was born there, she was too young to have made any memories. She was able to go to the house where she spent the first 18 months of her life. The family that lived in the house ignored the fact that we were complete strangers and welcomed us with open arms. Now our kids were experiencing genuine Indian hospitality to strangers. In addition to these visits, we also went to Jorhat in Assam to meet with our old family friend Dr. Kaul, who was now Vice Chancellor of the Assam Agriculture University, and to visit Kaziranga National Park. Last, we went to Goa, a former Portuguese colony on India's west coast that became part of independent India in the 1960s to celebrate New Year. The city is a big tourist destination due to its beautiful beaches and unique cuisine.

To fulfill our second purpose, our remarriage and recommitment, we married again in Chandigarh with a full Hindu ceremony, including saying seven oaths before a fire and circling the fire together after each oath. Many friends and family members attended. Although repeating wedding vows for a silver anniversary has become more popular in North America, it is quite rare in India for people to renew their vows, so we attracted some curious attention from the 100 or so guests. Family members and guests made speeches, and a memory album was created from photos. Our children not only witnessed their parents' recommitment to each other, but also the love and affection of the entire circle of family and friends.

Our personal experiences, our children's experiences, and the experiences of our friends and family members began to truly provide us with insights once we settled down and made our home. Only then, after becoming rooted, could we have those experiences to grow. Before our return to the U.S. in 1998, we had been absorbed in learning how to survive wherever we were, wrapped up in doing, with little time for reflection. Viney's hiring by Accenture, Kumud returning to health, starting the annual reunions, and becoming so involved in Chinmaya Mission all served to remove us from the life we had been living and transition us into a more enlightened outlook. Finding "our" place geographically and professionally opened our eyes to lessons about how we ought to order our lives.

- *Chart your own course, and the sky is the limit.* Taking risks is worthwhile when trying to remain secure leads to losing control of your destiny. Only you can know what you want to do and where you want to go. But the only thing you can change is you. Accept being a student all through life. Knowledge becomes stale if you don't pursue education every step of the way. Community service is essential to rounded personal growth. Giving back, participation in non-profit organizations, and taking leadership roles in charity events teach humility, respect, compassion, and teamwork.

- *Spirituality must become ingrained in your day to day lives.* Spiritual growth needs to be an ongoing pursuit as important as anything done to promote your professional career or strengthen personal relationships. Spirituality is not something to be learned after retirement. Putting off exploring your spirituality means you are putting off using your entire being during your most active years. Practicing meditation or yoga early in the day, even for a short time, will have an effect on all of your activities the rest of the day. More involved activities like retreats or classes help you learn new techniques and meet others seeking a spiritual life.

- *Family comes before anything else.* Corporate America is brutal and nobody's friend. Work as long and hard as your boss expects, and all that hard work is no guarantee you will avoid being let go if there is any downturn. Capitalism exists to strip people of the value of their labor and maximize their productivity for as little cost as possible. Putting work first only leads to divorces, emotional problems, health issues, and alienation from other aspects of living. Work–life balance is critical. With luck, you can find work you enjoy, but honestly most people get very little out of their jobs other than a paycheck. Compare that to the rewards you receive from spending active, attentive time with family members.

Varun's Graduation –
Chicago, 2007

Megha's Graduation
Omaha, 2001

Chicago 2001
5K walk for Charity

Robert Arnett –
famous author of
'India Unveiled' book
Chicago, 2008

Viney and Kumud taking marriage vows again on their 25th marriage Anniversary in India; Portrayed as Ram and Sita during 2005 Chinmaya Mission Chicago play

Family in Chandigarh
2004
After Marriage vows
were completed

Celebrating 25th Marriage Anniversary
Scottish style - Edinburgh 2004

Megha – Vivek Marriage Parents
Chicago, 2009

Meetings with world leaders as member of Accenture leadership Faculty
- Collin Powell, U.S. Secretary of State (2001-05);
- F.W. de Clerk, ex-President of S. Africa and 1993 Joint Noble laureate with Nelson Mandela;
- Chris Patten, Last Governor of Hong Kong before handover to China in 1997

Sixth Interlude:
Scandinavia (1995-2008)

"There are no foreign lands. It is the traveler only who is foreign."
Robert Louis Stevenson

We visited Denmark, Norway, Sweden and Finland during different years between 1995 and 2008. On the earlier trips, it was interesting to see Scandinavian culture from the eyes of somebody who was visiting from the U.S. and had lived in the U.S. only for a few years. The contrasts in the business environment were particularly interesting, having just gotten a grasp of U.S. business culture. We had many official meetings, and the locals were very relaxed, but meetings had to end by 5 p.m. The idea was for families to be together at meal times. If companies insist on people working longer hours, many employees just ignore the demand. We were told people rarely worked on weekends.

While the U.S. is very competitive and employers very demanding, the thinking in Scandinavian countries is work is a way to make money so one can enjoy one's spare time. Most people wanted to work just 37.5 hours per week. While in Norway, we heard they were thinking of further reducing the work week to 30 hours from the current average of 34 hours. Needless to say, strong labor unions help to support ideas like this. While their work weeks are already short, we heard a new term in Sweden called "squeeze days." These are the days before major holidays. Employees start thinking a few days before that they are already on holidays. In summer, they even have "squeeze weeks" leading up to the long vacations people take.

The wage differences between different categories were not that wide compared to the U.S. We talked to a waitress in a restaurant in Sweden and asked her how much she made. It was over $45K with tips. An IT consultant made $80K. In the U.S., waitresses make only $25K, and an IT professional could make as much as $150K. Once, we tipped a bartender, and it was funny to see her expression, as if she had been insulted. We were told tipping is not very common in bars, but you could tip in a restaurant if the service was very good. Wages in Denmark are high to make tips unnecessary. Other places add a 10 percent service charge, and that's it.

As indicated by a waitress willing to discuss her wages, the people were generally open up to a point. While they warm up to visitors after initial hesitation, we got the feeling there was a natural fear towards immigrants. Getting to really know people requires patience. We were told one needs to be persistent to make friends. On the other hand, Scandinavians seem to be more liberal with regard to social situations. Drinking is common, especially in Finland. Nudity was not an issue. Many pools and saunas had only nude people. Couples often have separate friends and go off for drinks, meals, whatever without their spouse/partner.

While in Copenhagen, we were told it is the world's happiest city. It seemed so, even though it was dark at 4 p.m. and the day had just started at 10 a.m. in winter. Of course, summer days stretch in some places from 4 a.m. to 11 p.m. One of the reasons for that happiness is caused by a reason for being unhappy. Our office staff in Sweden complained the income taxes were very high at nearly 60 percent. This created less motivation to push too hard for advancement, but there was little worry of being let go either. Viney asked what benefits they received from paying these high taxes. They could not deny they had excellent social, educational, and medical services. Education, for example, is globally-oriented, with children starting English and German very early on. Free home care is provided to mothers for a few days after childbirth. In Finland, the schools had no entrance exams, no fees. If a society's purpose is to help citizens become happy and fulfilled, these countries excel.

Seventh Interlude:
Latin America (1996-2006)

"Travel is fatal to prejudice, bigotry, and narrow-mindedness."
Mark Twain

Viney took a few business trips to Brasilia, São Paulo, and Buenos Aires. Here are his observations:

Brazilians and Argentinians are much more laid back than most business people in the United States. In the U.S., there is a "go-getter" attitude that promotes diligence and multitasking. Those I met in South America avoid expending energy or juggling tasks. Things get done, but without the pressure and anxiety. For example, time value has a different meaning in Latin America. Once, our meeting in São Paulo was scheduled from 9 a.m. to 3 p.m. It started at 10 and concluded at 5 p.m. I was told it is not abnormal in Brazil to start late and finish late. No one won points for being punctual at either end of a meeting. Completing the agenda was all that mattered. We had a contract to be signed. The company's representatives reviewed every minute detail and took hours and hours discussing those details and, after making many changes, agreeing.

For such a large, populous country, it was interesting that every Brazilian spoke Portuguese, one national language. Similarly, Spanish was the universal language in Argentina, even though it is an immigrant society like Canada or the U.S. (for example, Pope Francis from Argentina had Italian parents). Getting business done could appear chaotic, but not due to language difficulties. In Buenos Aires, the meetings had a lot of discussion and arguments and ended with no decisions being made. We were told the real power to make decisions was with superiors who were not there. In Brazil, people were interrupting each other all the time in meetings, and nobody cared. On the other hand, identifying an individual for criticism in a meeting was definitely not appreciated or welcome. One of my U.S. colleagues criticized a Brazilian employee. The reaction in the room was negative; my colleague had crossed the line to rudeness.

149

Moreover, the criticized employee had lost face in front of the others and chose not to turn up for a social dinner that evening.

Brazil and Argentina strictly follow hierarchy at work. No one would deign to use an open door policy or attempt to be inclusive of or friendly with members of the lower ranks. I found status in the workplaces was represented in their dress etiquette. The higher the position in the company, the finer and better dressed the person. What is funny is that it was similar to the sumptuary laws in European courts. No one but the monarch could wear cloth of gold or a few other rich cloths, no one but the dukes and duchesses could wear cloth of silver and a few more fine items, and so on. The best thing to do was to get to know the best dressed person you could find. It was critical for me to develop personal relationships with the executives first to win their loyalty and friendship. Doing so established my credibility within the company. Regrettably, like India, Brazil has a class system based on not only economic status, but also skin color. The executives put those expensive clothes on comparatively lighter skin.

Brazilians and Argentinians have a much better work-life balance like the Europeans than employees in the U,S. For our Argentina visit, we were specifically requested not to go during the months of January and February. It is summer in the Southern hemisphere, and these are holiday months for everyone. The social dinner after a meeting in Brazil was not unusual. People in both countries are friendly and like to socialize with colleagues. Once in Buenos Aires, I was invited for dinner to the home of one of my co-workers. I was told to arrive at 8 p.m. I arrived at 8 p.m. They were surprised I arrived at 8 p.m. I was surprised they were surprised I was so punctual. Later, I found out that "punctual" in Argentina means arriving 30-60 minutes late for dinners. Unfortunately, I also discovered a small gift or flowers are expected for the hostess. However, I learned of my mistake and sent her flowers the next day, as advised by a few friends. The gesture was appreciated and my lapse forgiven.

My visits to Argentina and Brazil were brief. However, the singularity of Latin American cultures is so striking, I couldn't help but take away a couple of insights.

- *Personal relationship building is critical.* Understanding the local work culture is very important for success anywhere. North America, East Asia, the Middle East, and Europe have been in the international business game long enough that their cultural variations are well known. Argentina and Brazil are emerging as more active participants. While it is always in one's interest to work with the right contacts to be successful, establishing friendships with the most senior people is flat out essential in South America. Since being called "networking", one might think someone on Wall Street invented the concept in the 1980s. In fact, developing personal relationships with prospective business partners has probably been around since commerce began. Think of Christopher Columbus spending so much time with the King of Portugal, and then the Queen of Castile and Leon. The New World was opened to Europeans by a man who persistently developed a bond until the other person had enough faith in him to agree to the deal.
- *Balance is critical.* Brazilians and Argentinians often work and socialize with the same people, particularly visitors. But work is for the work day. Dinner invitations are to allow the host to evaluate the guest's personality, to become better acquainted; they are not additional business meetings. Life is give and take, little adjustments to stay balanced. If the workday ends later than usual, perhaps one goes in a bit later the next day. One's family is supreme. Loved ones take precedence over all else. Vacations are fixed. They are not determined by if and when one can get away.

Singapore (2010-13)

"If you come to a fork in the road, take it."
Yogi Berra

In June 2010, Viney was approached by Accenture leadership. They asked him to consider a leadership role in the Asia-Pacific region in their office based in Singapore, Malaysia, or India. We discussed the idea as a family. We did not want to move again. Viney wondered whether he could perform the duties while based in Chicago. That would mean extensive and frequent travel to the area, with entire days eaten up just going one way or the other. When he proposed this option, Viney was told the role required his physical presence somewhere in the region.

Kumud in particular was not in favor of moving again, a reasonable antipathy given her experience in Delhi. Toward the end of July, we were in a wedding in Ohio. The trip gave us a lot of free time to discuss the position again. Kumud relented just to the point of agreeing to consider the idea. As we had done in the past, we reviewed the pros and cons. Aside from the practical and emotional arguments for and against, two questions kept popping up that we always had answered "yes" when making decisions in the past. Do we want to jump at this opportunity? Isn't this just destiny working in our lives again?

We had tossed the idea around for so long, three additional contenders for the role were under consideration by the time Viney said he wanted to consider the position. He was considered the best of the lot in terms of experience and management's number one choice. The company offered Viney the role in September 2010 with the expectation we would move to Singapore by the end of October. By mid-October, we had packed most of the house when the global leader to whom the role reported called and said our move was not approved by leadership, that it was either on hold or cancelled altogether. We were supposed to be leaving in two days for Singapore to make pre-transfer arrangements.

Viney can never forget the support of his immediate business leader, Dave Rich, who stood up to management and made them change their mind. He had as much seniority in the company as the guy who said no. He sent a very aggressive message to management saying our guy is all set, house ready to be rented, all their furniture and household items in storage, etc. The global leader who had said no believed that a local Asian executive would be as good for the position as someone from North America. However, he now fully understood the logic of sending Viney from the global alliance leadership team rather than hiring a local and relented. The role just needed someone with deep connections to the global leadership team and a proven track record, both of which Viney had.

Kumud and Viney made the pre-transfer trip around October 20, 2010, to look at accommodations and transportation, along with attending an orientation to Singapore by the company for expatriates and families. We received a very thorough presentation on culture and other aspects of how to conduct ourselves while working in Singapore. After the one-day orientation, we had three days looking for housing, furniture companies, cars, and other logistical details.

From the beginning, this experience had not been smooth, and it continued to be bumpy. On our return to Chicago from the pre-transfer trip, Kumud got cold feet and said she did not want to go to Singapore anymore. Regardless, we were too far ahead in our packing and planning. Cancellation of the trip was not an option. Megha and Varun were instrumental in convincing their mother to go, and Kumud reluctantly agreed to give it a go. We reached Singapore on November 7, 2010, for a three-year assignment.

We had made arrangements to stay in the Marriott the first week because the condo wasn't available until November 15. We arrived in Singapore at 1 a.m. It was quickly apparent that we had too much luggage for one cab. We were in a dilemma. Should we take two cabs at one o'clock in the morning? Reluctantly, we agreed to do that. The drivers of both the cabs understood our dilemma and were smiling. Then one of them said, "Sir, this is Singapore – the safest place on Earth. You should not worry." He was so right. This is exactly what we found during our three-year stay in Singapore. There even was a running joke. The wife protects the man's honor when couples are out in the streets.

Our settlement was fast. We moved into the condo we had chosen on schedule. Being a country with very little land, apartments in high rise buildings are the most typical form of housing. Rents are very high due to demand and quality. We paid S$7,500 (US$6,000) per month for a 1485 square foot condo with three bedrooms. We certainly could not afford it if the company wasn't helping. Given how limited land was, apartments could be easily as big as or bigger than a house. About 80 percent of Singapore residents live in flats, with the rent subsidized by the government. The residential towers are efficient. Expats go for the buildings that have swimming pools, fitness rooms, etc.

Lux flats all have a room and bathroom for a live-in staff person. Domestic help is common among expats and wealthier citizens. Most household staff employees are Malay, Burmese, or Thai. They usually do everything: cooking, cleaning, childcare. We just had someone come in once a week to help with cleaning, so the room was left vacant. There was no justification for us to have a live-in maid.

All of the furniture, bedding, etc. we had purchased arrived the day we moved in. Before long, we had obtained all the items needed for running a household, and we were fully operational by the end of November. The transition was far easier compared to Iraq and Saudi Arabia. Of course, Canada had been a slow process waiting for the shipped goods. Even our move to the U.S. required more effort, even with the company's help.

Singapore is a wonderful city-state, impossible not to fall in love with. Everything is very clean, more so even than Canada. With many expats and well-paid residents, European and U.S. store chains are plentiful and malls are everywhere. We have never seen as many Louis Vuitton stores in one city as we saw in Singapore, and all were doing a roaring business. One could easily see lots of Singaporean women with expensive Louis Vuitton purses. On enquiry, we were told most Singaporeans can't buy a condo or car, as the prices are out of reach. This is just a way to satisfy their material desires.

All types of food are available, which makes Singapore a much easier place to eat compared to countries that only serve their own country's food and fast food. Most Singaporeans go to Hawker

Centers that are in every locality. Food peddlers are directed to set up in designated areas so they aren't scattered around on street corners like they are in Manhattan and elsewhere. Their ingredients are subsidized, so they make fresh food in front of you for $5 or less. Families and couples find it is far easier for each person to get whatever he or she wants rather than everyone eating the same food of a home-cooked meal. Fresh juices made from almost any fruit or vegetable are everywhere. Restaurants are not too expensive if one prefers less public dining.

Eating out is almost far too common. When we first saw our flat, Kumud asked why the kitchen was so clean, it looked brand new. She was told Singaporeans don't cook at home, so the kitchen appliances never get dirty. We found every item from the U.S., Europe, and India available in the grocery. Food was reasonably priced, but everything else was so expensive. Kumud is certain the only items we purchased in three years were food.

The entire place is easy to navigate. The public transportation system is absolutely wonderful, probably the best in the world. One can easily do without a car. Since the country is so small, a trip is never longer than 45 minutes. Cabs were all over. The drivers were honest and knowledgeable about politics and economics in many different countries. They seemed to enjoy conversing with passengers about everything and learned as a result. Despite the transport system, we had a car leased by the company. It was a new Toyota Camry, and the lease was S$2,900 (U.S.$2,300) per month. The sale price for a new Toyota Camry was S$125,000 (U.S.$100,000). That was not the manufacturer's fault. Singapore enforces a quota on how many vehicles can be put on the road. The government collects an entitlement fee permitting someone to have a car. That fee makes up about two-thirds the cost of the vehicle.

Both the airport and Singapore Airlines are considered the best in the world. When first constructed, the airport became a model for all others. Now, with rebuilding, everyone will have something new to emulate. U.S. airlines can't even compare to Singapore Airlines on any level, particularly service. On a trip to Tokyo in business class, Viney asked for some champagne 45 minutes before landing. The stewardess opened a fresh bottle to satisfy his request. And with such a wonderful airport, Singapore is the gateway to the whole of

Asia and the Pacific. Going to any of the many neighboring countries is a cinch. A flight to India took only five hours. Being so close and having so many flights, we found it easy to stay in touch with the many relatives that still lived in our motherland.

Sitting almost on the equator, Singapore's climate is tropical: hot, but not intolerably so due to rain cooling things down. It is consistently rated as the best East Asian country in terms of quality of life and one of the top 20 cities in the world. One factor that certainly stands out is the diversity, blending Asian values with Western liberalization. The country is home to a variety of cultures from different parts of the world. English, Chinese, Malay, and Tamil are all official languages. However, Singlish, the local version of English, seems to be used most often, even though it is sometimes difficult to understand.

Some small sections are known for their concentration of people from one culture, and everyone joins in to celebrate the festivals of those cultures. Little India is decorated lavishly for Diwali, even better than in India. The decorations stay up for a month and a half. The same occurs in the Chinese market area for Chinese New Year. All religious communities exist harmoniously with temples, mosques, and churches throughout the territory. Everyone wants to stay, so everyone gets along with others who have the same feeling. The expat community isn't just large; it contains many long-timers.

Singapore has appeared more often in foreign news due to its strict approach to illegal drugs. Death for Drug Trafficking is written in block letters on the back of every visa form. The government means it. They do indeed execute people for drug possession, even foreigners. This draconian policy has kept Singapore virtually drug-free. On a more pleasant note, the Formula One race is a major draw in Singapore. It is the only race on the circuit that is run at night. Singapore is closed during the third week of September for people to enjoy it.

Although small, Singapore always aims to provide the best resources. Higher education is given a lot of importance, as exemplified by the quality of National University of Singapore, Nanyang Technological University, and the European INSEAD MBA program. Healthcare is just as high in quality and very efficient; doctor visits are affordable and hospital costs not too high.

156

Recreation abounds in the form of museums, movie theaters, amusement parks, and Universal Studios.

Once one has exhausted all of the fun activities in Singapore, one can drive to Malaysia or make a quick visit to Indonesia, Thailand, and other countries in the southeast and east of Asia. However, we always needed to remember that we were leaving tolerant Singapore. In a cab in Malaysia, Viney mentioned about Osama bin Laden having been killed. The cabbie became agitated, saying the U.S. should not have done it and the U.S. was evil. We realized too late that we were in a Muslim country. We should have known better. Many years earlier in Iraq, Viney had mentioned to a Pakistani co-worker about why a woman's testimony in court is only worth half of a man's. The man told Viney that is a rule in sharia and Viney had no business disputing what other people believed as part of their faith. In a friendly way, he advised Viney not to make any religious comments since many Muslim friends will take offence.

Interactions in our travels usually were more congenial. We became hooked on the inexpensive massages available in all of the neighboring countries. We also became hooked on fresh carrot juice in Singapore. When he wasn't travelling, Viney was able to work from home about 60 percent of the time, just as he had been doing in the U.S. His office hours were virtually 24 hours since North America woke up when the Asia Pacific region was sleeping and he had to have almost daily interactions with leadership and other teams in North America. Almost every day, around 4 or 5 in the afternoon, we would drive to Holland Village Hawker Centre for carrot juice. The vendors got to know us so well that if we skipped a day, they would ask why we didn't come the day before. If Viney went by himself while Kumud was in India visiting relatives, they would ask, "Where is Kumud? We haven't seen her."

Viney's office was located in a large mall connected to the MRT, Singapore's primary mass transit system. The trip was only 25 minutes from home to office. Viney's position was a key part of the alliance function he was leading for Accenture in the Asia-Pacific region. During his three years, a lot of progress was made on the alliances front. He hired at least 40 new team members in nine different Asia Pacific countries. The senior management at global as well as regional levels praised his performance on all fronts. Even better, his team of 50 people really appreciated his leadership, the team spirit he promoted within the group, and his genuine, people-oriented actions. All in all, the stint was an outstanding success.

More than 50 percent of the time, Viney was traveling to other countries, looking after alliances. Aside from Singapore, he was responsible for activities in Malaysia, Indonesia, Thailand, the Philippines, India, China, Hong Kong, Taiwan, Japan, South Korea, and Australia. He traveled to these countries frequently. Kumud was able to go with Viney the first or second time he had a business trip somewhere. Sometimes, she was able to return to a country for another visit. Kumud would find a tour guide while Viney went to the office. A special and memorable treat was Kumud's personal driver in China who spoke English. They were able to talk freely about China and other subjects. Just think what the Saudi *muttawas* would have said about a woman driving around with an unrelated man!

Actually, more than anything else, these trips fulfilled Viney's promise to Kumud before going to Singapore that they would visit 15 new countries together. Singapore and India didn't count since we had been to both. Each trip, we would say one down, fourteen to go, or seven down, eight to go. When our three years were almost up, time was running out for us. We had visited 14 countries. It would be so frustrating to miss fulfilling the promise by one. We scheduled a quick trip to New Zealand and succeeded.

Singapore really suited Kumud from many angles, not just because she was able to explore other countries. She was also able to visit family in India more than ten times during those three years and was able to attend all the major festivals and marriages during that time. Kumud had plenty of quality time with Viney since he worked from home so much when he wasn't traveling. She was able to indulge in many activities like learning Mandarin and wandering among the many colorful markets with another expatriate family and friends from Chicago. She also attended naturopathy sessions for 10-15 days in Bangalore three times, once with an American Indian friend. The best activity above all others, though, was driving with Viney every afternoon to drink fresh carrot juice.

Unlike the difficulties Kumud faced when we tried living in Delhi, her health was even better than at home in Chicago. The consistently hot climate eradicated any trace of her arthritis. She rarely needed to visit doctors, going only about 25 percent as much compared to in the U.S. Visits to physicians also were more pleasant and less time consuming. Doctors kept appointment times religiously, unlike in the U.S., where doctors are always overbooked and patients invariably wait up to an hour past the scheduled time. In addition to providing vaccinations for malaria and other tropical diseases, doctors dispensed medicines directly rather than writing prescriptions to be taken to a pharmacy. We definitely preferred Singapore's medical system over that in the U.S.

Most of our family members and friends from India, England, the U.S., and Canada visited us in Singapore and stayed with us from one week to one month. Most of our weekends were spent entertaining guests. For all of them, we made a customized itinerary before their arrival, and we followed each schedule religiously. These pre-planned schedules were a huge success, and all of our guests still remember how productive their visits had been due to our preparations. Kumud took the responsibility of escorting guests. She had a preferred cabbie in Penang whenever she took guests to Malaysia. Singapore was one place where we could entertain guests very well and even take them to nearby countries like Malaysia, Thailand, and Indonesia. One standard item for all guests was listed as a pedicure by beautiful ladies. Imagine their surprise when they found out the beautiful ladies were the residents of a fish spa. The fish delicately eat the dead skin from your feet, creating a delightful, tingling sensation. One could dangle your feet in a pool with larger fish initially and then switch to a pool containing smaller fish that would offer a more refined feeling.

One might think that our three years in Singapore drinking carrot juice, getting massages, and visiting the fish spa dulled us into not seeing how the miracle of the city-state offered lessons for our continuing education in how important a global perspective is. Quite the contrary. Singapore had benefited from the strong and benevolent leadership of long time Prime Minister Lee Kwon Yew, who was able to consistently pursue policies that established the country as a major international business hub and refused to allow the diverse communities to ever feel as though they had to compete for resources. As a result, Singapore is perhaps the most relaxing place in the world in which to conduct business.

Embracing diversity and encouraging inclusiveness creates a stable environment. In 1966, a year after Singapore left the Malay Confederation, talk started about a national language. The Chinese majority wanted Mandarin. However, making standard Chinese the official language would make Malays, Tamils, Westerners, and other minorities feel like second-class citizens. Moreover, if Singapore was going to develop economically with virtually no resources other than its location and its people, the prime minister argued that English, the language of world commerce, must be embraced. Singapore would need to attract some immigrants to fill roles citizens weren't trained for yet. Immigration would be stymied if English was not used. The government intended on creating a meritocracy that would place skill and ability above ethnic ties and make corruption unnecessary. The government would build a middle class society in which foreigners helped speed development. As a result, locals don't resent foreigners; they see expats as allies, a part of a country striving to excel. Immigrants aren't taking their jobs. They are just filling positions that are difficult to fill with a small population. Above all, harmony, as represented by the many religious festivals celebrated with equal fervor throughout the year, is essential.

- *Think strategically and plan for long-term goals.* Singapore started out knowing it had good workers and a solid location. The people happily embraced Lee Kwon Yew's autocratic vision with elections that gave his party 90 percent of the vote. Plans required that buildings were architecturally ahead of their time and built well enough to be useful for many decades. Even now, the same ideals hold sway. Plans for a new airport are far beyond any others being considered in the world. Affordable housing and decent jobs were needed to allow citizens to be middle class consumers. Even something as mundane as tipping was addressed, with 10 percent automatically added to restaurant bills and taxi rates set to include tips. Housing needed

160

to rise vertically in order to preserve as much of the country's natural beauty as possible. All of this work turned Singapore into a large economy on a very small base. Singapore became so attractive, companies from elsewhere could not pass up using it as a center of operations for that quadrant of the world. Today, there are regional offices of more than 4,000 global companies in Singapore. It is one the largest financial hubs in the region, going head to head with Hong Kong.

- *Safety in a primarily urban state is paramount.* Singapore ranks among the safest countries on Earth. Kumud experienced so much without any concern. We saw women travel everywhere at any time. Singapore's success in maintaining public safety primarily is the threat of severe punishment and the very public prosecution of alleged criminals. For example, prostitution is legal, but only if the prostitute is 18 or older. A 17-year-old call girl was discovered. However, she was treated more as a victim of crime. The 48 men who had paid her for sex, however, had their names published in the newspaper when charged, and they were all prosecuted for having sex with an underage female. Just like any sordid case like this, some of the men involved were somewhat prominent, including a school principal, a police superintendent, and a high-ranked UBS bank officer.

Manila, Philippines 2013

Traditional Japanese
Outfit
Tokyo - 2012

Singapore Bird Park 2012

With Varun
Jaipur, Rajasthan, India 2015

Eighth Interlude:
East Asia (2011-12)

"A journey is like marriage. The certain way to be wrong is to think you control it."
John Steinbeck

Japan is one of the most pleasant countries to visit, even though it is a little expensive and crowded. The Tokyo subway system is one of the best and most punctual in the world. However, it can be a little daunting to get one's bearings at the stations. Once we were at one of the Tokyo subway stations and wanted to walk to our hotel, which we knew was only one mile away. We asked a young Japanese gentleman for directions. He said not to worry, I will take you there. He started leading us towards the hotel. When our hotel was only a couple of minutes away and in sight, he said I will take leave and started walking in the same direction we had just come from. We were surprised and asked him where he was going. He said his place was exactly the opposite direction of the subway station. He had walked with us for 15 minutes to only make us reach our hotel safely. How great is that?

We were told many stories about the honesty of Japanese people. If, by chance, somebody forgets something in the subway, even a wallet, nobody will touch it. The item will stay safe there until either the person comes back, which is unlikely, or a train employee finds it and deposits the item with the lost and found department, where the person can collect it from there. Unlikely? Spend even a short time in Japan, and one sees many courtesies not found elsewhere. Small incidents show the character of a nation and the Buddhist culture behind that character.

For example, Kumud made friends with one of the staff at the ANA InterContinental Hotel where we were staying. Kumud made plans with her to see Tokyo. They decided to meet outside a subway station. Kumud reached the station at the appointed time and found there were five exits. She had no idea which of the five exits she should take to go out. Each exit went in a different direction. Kumud was totally confused, and it was apparent. A Japanese lady approached her and asked if she could help since Kumud seemed confused. Kumud shared her predicament. Luckily, Kumud had the telephone number of her contact. The stranger called the person and stayed with Kumud for 20 minutes until they found Kumud's friend from the hotel at the proper spot. Then the stranger went back into the station to get on her way. Even though there are many language schools throughout the country, many Japanese don't speak English or don't understand it well enough. The lady who saw Kumud standing not knowing which way to go clearly felt she should use her English language skills to be helpful.

Our son Varun recommended we visit some of the natural hot springs. During one of his visits to Japan, he had been greatly impressed by them. We had a wonderful experience. The springs are distinguished by the types of minerals dissolved in the water. Different minerals provide different health benefits. All hot springs are supposed to have a relaxing effect on your body and mind. We found that hot spring baths come in many varieties, indoors and outdoors, gender separated and mixed, developed and undeveloped. We went to world-famous Hakone, a two hour train ride from Tokyo. Men and women bathe on separate sides of the spring because one of the conditions is users must be completely naked. Viney made one mistake. Before going into a hot spring, one should take a bath. Viney did not know this and just walked straight out of the disrobing room in a towel. No one said anything as he entered the water with dry hair showing he had not bathed. Many eyes did look at him, the closest a Japanese person might go to show disapproval of a foreigner's actions. The thing is that Viney knew to take a shower before entering a swimming pool, but he thought the rule wasn't needed for hot springs. Sometimes, one learns something new at the expense of one's pride.

On the business front, Viney had a work team in Japan and also had meetings with high officials in many other companies. He learned quickly to have lots of business cards on hand. Business cards are an extension of the personality of a person. They are essential to know what position someone has, since Japanese business people are acutely aware of position. The appropriate method of giving and accepting cards is to use both hands. Since hierarchy is so well respected, we always ensured to show we were honored to be with the most senior person in the office. In meetings, silence is golden at times. A person has more credibility saying nothing than trying to participate too actively. Viney noticed no one ever clearly agreed or disagreed. Japan has a group-oriented culture. Individual achievements are less important than group success. Viney tried to follow suit despite being more used to livelier meetings.

For men, a business suit with a tie is the norm. For women, dresses are conservative, with only modest jewelry. A tall female employee confided in Viney that she could never wear heels to work. Her status was low, and she already was taller than some men. Using heels would make her look arrogant. This notion of making decisions for appearance's sake is widespread. Viney learned on his first trip that bowing to people one meets shows respect and earns points. It was a simple but helpful way to break the ice during an initial business meeting.

Even one's chopstick use and manners were noted. Demonstrating some proficiency helped to fit in. If one cannot grasp the use of chopsticks, restaurants will always provide Western cutlery since they want to be courteous and helpful to customers. However, showing one's gratitude by leaving a tip for the server who fetched that cutlery for you is rude. Pointing at people with one's fingers is terribly rude. Metaphorically pointing fingers in a group setting is equally rude. Shame is a critical element of Japanese culture, as in other East Asian cultures. Even constructive criticism should be provided in private.

The Japanese have come to love coffee over tea. Not all traditional tastes have been dumped, though. Sumo wrestling has remained Japan's national sport. We had the good fortune of seeing a high profile sumo match. The manner in which the combatants first demonstrate respect and then stay within formalized rules is unique. We also saw Tsukiji Fish Market in Tokyo, which is the largest wholesale fish and seafood market in the world and as proudly representative of Japan as sumo. Of course, the fish gets distributed and eaten. We went to a restaurant recommended by Varun where the seven-course meal was about $60-$70. Half of the courses were raw fish, another famed aspect of Japan. We didn't care for it, so the dinner seemed overpriced to us. We discovered that horse meat is liked in Japan and is served raw in thin slices, like beef carpaccio. Still, with Buddhism as the main religion, the Japanese are quite capable of making vegetarian meals. Most hotels have Buddhist religious books in the drawers, just like the Gideon Bibles in hotels in the U.S.

Japan usually appears quite modern, especially in large cities like Tokyo, with its distinctive skyscrapers and the latest technologies displayed in the Ginza shopping district. Reminders of tradition and the past are sometimes tucked away, but they can be as prominent as the enormous moat and grounds surrounding the Imperial Palace in the middle of Tokyo that annoy drivers because they must circle around. One of the quirkier traditions is to display realistic plastic versions of the dishes served in noodle shops and small restaurants. This helps foreigners because they can choose what looks good in the window, and if necessary, an employee will go out to the display so the foreigner can point out the desired dish.

The Japanese people seem to have made their lives quite livable by many measures. They are near the top of rankings among developed countries for education and healthcare. That latter is evident from the fact that Japan has the highest proportion of elderly people in the world. Amazingly, 23 percent of Japanese people are over the age of 65. The Japanese also can be proud, were they not so modest, that the literacy rate is almost 100 percent and the homicide rate is the lowest in the world.

All in all, Japan is a great society. We rate it very close to the top on the list of places where we had the most positive experiences, a close contender with Singapore and New Zealand. A few characteristics particularly struck us as being profound ways Japan and the Japanese excel.

- *A hierarchical system in business and family produces many positive results.* The modern world often seems chaotic, with no one knowing what is top or bottom, left or right. Almost every society has been hierarchical sometime in its history. Sometimes that can be exclusionary, granting men or landowners authority that women and landless people can never obtain. However,

Japan has an organic hierarchy. Those at the top got there by being patient and learning as they grew older or rose through the ranks of a company. The old in Japan are honored and revered. Why? Simply because they were born longer ago and therefore have more experience living than younger people. Except for becoming emperor, anyone in Japan can rise to any position

- *Buddhism is a philosophy of action.* Originating in India, Buddhism spread quite far without leaders conquering territories and converting the population. It spread because people understood the wisdom of Buddhist teachings, particularly the paradox of removing one's interests from interactions with others to promote one's interests. This philosophy has had a profound impact on the Japanese people. They are extremely modest and helpful, expecting no reward for acting charitably. They respect the idea that whatever does not belong to you, you do not take. Buddhism has taught the Japanese that their actions determine who they are, a great lesson.

We had many visits to Beijing and Shanghai during 2011-2013. China and India have been rivals since the 1950s, initially over borders and since 1980 in the world economy. They are both large countries, each with more than one billion people, together close to one-third of the world's entire population. China is the larger with 1.3 billion people, but India is expected to pass China by 2030. The reason is China's one-child policy that was recently changed to permit more couples to have two children. After over three decades, there are now 32 million more boys than girls in China; as adults, these male children might have a hard time getting brides. Presumably, the imbalance will be corrected by the two-child policy as parents become less likely to end pregnancies if the child will be a girl. The policy was never popular because of the cultural desirability of a boy to carry on the family name and be better able to provide aid to elderly parents. However, the policy helped control the strain on resources from a fast-growing population and freed those resources for the economic boom.

Authoritarian governments, like China's one-party system, sometimes are criticized for imposing policies that are unpopular but which the authorities believe are in the greater interest of everyone.

We saw this in Iraq and Singapore. Saddam Hussein was a monster, particularly toward the Kurds. However, his firm grip meant that the Shi'a and Sunni Arabs in the country had to get along. Al-Qaeda had no operations or known support in Iraq until after his government was toppled. Then it transformed into the Islamic State.

Although China has as many ethnic communities as India, Han people, what the Chinese call their selves, make up about 95 percent of China's population. This is due to China having been united for centuries at a time off and on since 221 BCE, giving the Han the opportunity to spread in all directions at the expense of fringe communities. Due to the Han being such a large majority, the one-child policy never applied to ethnic minorities. One dominant empire on the entire Indian subcontinent has never happened, although the Mughal Empire came close. Britain united the various kingdoms and principalities in India under colonial rule just in 1857. For that matter, aside from Japan taking control of China bit by bit, starting with Manchuria in 1931, China was not a colony of any country. However, as a result of losing the Opium Wars in the mid-1800s, China was forced to allow European and U.S. merchants to live in many coastal cities in areas where Chinese laws did not apply. The only two outright colonies in China were Hong Kong and Macau.

Just as India started looking for foreign economic partners in the 1990s, China did the same even earlier, starting in 1981. The goal was to expand national productivity using foreign investments. The method was to allow local officials to sign agreements worth up to certain amounts without approval from the central government. Then, individuals were allowed to start their own businesses and villages regained control of what they wanted to produce above and beyond the food needed for the villagers. The transformation in China still seems miraculous. In about 30 years, China has created a middle class that is equal in size to the entire population of the United States, more than 300 million people. The people in that growing middle class want all kinds of consumer products. Growing demand has fed growing production. One result was that businesses in China needed consultants, so companies like Accenture arrived. Viney had a large Chinese team in China and interacted with them frequently.

We learned all kinds of fun and interesting facts during our many visits that proved extremely valuable:

Chinese New Year is an enormous national festival and celebration that lasts for up to two weeks. So many people travel to their home counties to be with family, it rivals the hajj as one of the largest annual migrations of humans. While people from all over the world go to one place, Makkah, for the hajj, the Chinese go in all directions within their own country for the New Year. The Chinese zodiac consists of 12 animals: Rat, Ox, Tiger, Rabbit, Dragon, Snake, Horse, Sheep, Monkey, Rooster, Dog, and Pig. Each year reflects the characteristics of whatever animal is dedicated to that year, e.g. 2016 will be the Year of the Monkey. However, the Chinese use a lunar calendar, and the New Year begins sometime in late January to mid-February, so the first few weeks of 2016, until February 8, are still part of the Year of the Sheep.

China does everything on a large scale. The country's most famous icon is the Great Wall, a structure that runs from the Yellow Sea for thousands of miles into the Gobi desert. It began as a series of walls built by individual kingdoms that were pieced together by the first emperor to unite all of the kingdoms. Some dynasties took better care of it than others. The last dynasty to rebuild it to keep northern invaders out was the Ming. The mortar used to bind the Great Wall's stones was made with sticky rice, of all things! Still, it was an effective defense against assault, but not treachery.

A Ming general was bribed to open one of the gates to the Manchurians. They occupied Beijing, and the last Ming emperor hung himself on Coal Hill behind the Forbidden City. The Manchurians set up the Qing dynasty. They had no use for the wall since their homeland was on the other side of the wall, and it fell into disrepair again. The Communists won the civil war in 1949 that had essentially begun when the last Qing emperor abdicated in 1912. They eventually recognized the value of restoring parts of the wall accessible from Beijing to attract both domestic and foreign tourists. Tourists who climb far enough can get past the recently built parts and walk on sections actually built in the 1400s. And bolder tourists who travel on the old Silk Road to western China can see the remains of the very end of the Wall and the farthest fortification of the empire, both built around 220 BCE. However, they won't be seeing much sticky rice, as the Wall that far out was just made from bricks made of mud and straw.

Another huge icon of China is the Forbidden City in Beijing. An immense area with thick, towering, ochre walls surrounded by a moat contains 9,000 rooms. This was the palace complex built by the Ming dynasty and designed to reflect their view of the universe on an auspicious north-south axis. Three huge courtyards separate three great, raised halls along the axis. The last hall contains the emperor's throne with golden cushions. Carved five-toed dragons, a symbol of the emperor, are everywhere. The precincts on the western side contain the apartments of the emperor, his wives and concubines, his mother, the Empress Dowager (who might not be his mother), and his children. China proudly displays many of the fascinating machines, toys to us, made for the emperor's amusement, as well as examples of the furniture and art typical of the rooms.

Viney observed many things in official and social settings. A visitor is always expected to arrive on time or early for meetings. Formal titles must be used during introductions, and as usual, business cards are presented with both hands. The decision-making process was very slow. One must be mentally prepared for many rounds of talks before reaching a decision. Any kind of impatience is unacceptable. The Chinese value rank and title, so the most important matters must be saved to discuss with senior executives who will make the decisions.

Gift giving is a very delicate issue in China. The most acceptable gift is a banquet. A Chinese banquet takes place around a large, round table with a lazy Susan in the center. At least a dozen dishes featuring all kinds of meats and vegetables are placed on the turning platform. Some platters may contain just stir-fried mushrooms or another individual item. Others have a mixture of ingredients cut into small pieces, just as we are used to from Chinese restaurants in North America. However, the sauces are not usually as thick or abundant. Sometimes, it is difficult to tell what has been served, but visitors are expected to taste every dish at a banquet. Even though a banquet includes co-workers or clients, no business is discussed at meals.

Once, Kumud arranged for an exclusive tour guide for herself through the hotel we stayed at in Beijing. The guide was a local Chinese man who had studied in the UK. He spoke excellent English. He confided to Kumud that a majority of the people in China wished freedom of speech was adopted, but most are hesitant to raise their voice, lest they are targeted and punished. He said there are hundreds of websites that are blocked by the government. People end up forced to use Chinese email, shopping, and social media services. Some prominent blocked sites are Gmail, Google, Facebook, Picasa, Twitter, and Amazon. Kumud was upset that she could not open many of the sites she is used to surfing. Aside from the private discussions an English-speaking personal tour guide provides, this method of seeing a place as large as Beijing gives one the opportunity to linger where one likes and move on if something isn't interesting.

In Beijing and Shanghai, we were looking for a vegetarian restaurant. An expat chief scientist from Accenture and his wife, also from Chicago, took us to a vegetarian restaurant we will never forget. Pure Lotus Restaurant in Beijing is one of a kind. The staff members wore Buddhist monks' robes since they are actual monks, the menu was inscribed in wood, and the names of menu items are non-vegetarian, but every item is completely vegetarian, with the "meat" made from soya. Similarly in Shanghai, we were exposed to Godly Vegetarian Restaurant, another excellent restaurant. Like Lotus, all items were listed as non-vegetarian but were vegetarian. We were amused by this because it seemed odd to call dishes beef this and chicken that if the customer wants vegetarian food. Tipping is considered insulting.

Tea is synonymous with China and makes a nice souvenir or gift for someone at home. Lots of opportunities arose to taste teas from vendors and shops, but they made clear they expected us to pay. There are many areas for shopping, some that seem to be just for tourists and others that locals use. A group of Korean boys and girls visiting Shanghai thought Kumud was Chinese. It was not a surprise for us since she is often confused as one of the locals in most countries. It would have been helpful if one of us really was Chinese. We needed someone to explain to taxi drivers where to go, even when the address was written in Chinese characters. Perhaps GPS will catch on.

China is such a large country with a lot of diversity. However, the long periods of unification and the existence of one-party rule since 1949 also have created many commonalities. China is the only successful Communist country, but it has been so successful by providing a lot of economic freedom in the last 35 years. This unusual path, what Deng Xiaoping called "socialism with Chinese characteristics" when he started the policy, provides some very interesting lessons when seen through our experiences elsewhere.

- *Freedom is more precious if one sees societies that lack freedom.* Chinese people on paper have all kinds of freedoms, but the reality is that these supposed freedoms are severely limited. Essentially, people are free to do what they want so long as the government does not find it offensive or dangerous to social harmony. However, the government finds many things offensive or dangerous to social harmony, particularly anything that appears to question or criticize the government, policies and laws, or the Communist Party. Most people in North America and Europe do not value the freedom they have because it's there like the ground or air. Those who have gone to places like Saudi Arabia, Iraq, and China have seen freedom restricted. After that experience, they can no longer take freedom for granted.
- *Authoritarian societies often provide much-needed stability.* Unless the leadership is aggressive, as in Iraq under Saddam Hussein, or completely ignores the needs of citizens, as in North Korea, even dictators have positive qualities like maintaining peace and security or giving people the opportunity to focus on economic gains. The Chinese Communist government has done both of these things since 1980. Hundreds of millions of citizens have benefited. A good comparison is Singapore from 1968 to the 1980s. Lee Kwon Yew ruled the city-state like a dictator. After all, the citizens had no say in their government when it was a British colony. Singapore became extremely wealthy thanks to his good management and positive policies. Then he relaxed his grip and let the country become a democratic society, but one

that already was attending to the needs of the people. The problem with autocratic rule arises primarily when it curbs basic human rights. If there is at least some outlet for dissenters to challenge the government, the idea of political discourse isn't brand new once progress makes authoritarian rule unneeded.

China and Hong Kong is like a marriage of convenience between communism and capitalism. The interesting contrast is described by the official name for the relationship: one country, two systems. The British colonial legacy and influence are still there, even though the territory has been under Chinese rule since 1997. Skyscrapers have been the norm for decades due to shortage of land. Hong Kong is the skyscraper capital of the world, having more than any other city in the world.

While doing business, British etiquette is still common. Plain, dark suits are the business uniform for both men and women. Punctuality and hierarchy count. Chinese business people want to feel comfortable with your personality before talking business, so the conversation begins with informal topics. Business relationships are started with the long view in mind. Like in other Asian countries, silence is as important as words in business dealings and business cards given with both hands and the typeface turned toward the receiver are extremely critical. Also as elsewhere, shame is a big deal. Viney ensured not to provide any constructive feedback to people in front of others. The Hong Kong experiences were more like conducting meetings in the UK, with two exceptions. Astrology and other traditional practices are followed for important decisions. Also, the influence of Buddhism is as great as the large bronze statue, the Big Buddha, constructed in 1993.

Macau has the same kind of history and relationship to China as Hong Kong, but they are more unlike each other than alike. Macau is easily reached by jet foil ferry crossing the mouth of the Pearl River from Hong Kong to Macau. On arrival, all immigration processes are followed. One is treated like you are entering a new country, even though you have just gone from one part of China to another. Macau was established by the Portuguese as a colony long before the British obtained Hong Kong and returned it to China in

1999, two years after Hong Kong. We could still see Portuguese influences in the old architecture. Nonetheless, Chinese culture predominates.

The territory has been infamous for money laundering and shady deals involving China, made easier as it became the Casino Capital of the World after overtaking Las Vegas. All of the major casinos have set up operations: Sands, Plaza, Venetian, Marina, MGM, Wynn, etc. We were told 40 percent of the revenue for the country was from casinos. The funny thing is that all of this gambling activity was built from just a couple of casinos that were around when the Portuguese left. The communists, not the capitalists, created this gambling mecca.

Hong Kong and Macau are fascinating relics of colonialism tethered to huge China but retaining very distinctive identities. The residents follow basic Chinese cultural rules, not surprisingly since 95 percent of the people are ethnically Chinese. However, those rules fit within unusual East-West hybrid entities. Their uniqueness offers unique lessons.

- *Sometimes a place is a worthwhile destination for no reason except it exists.* We had no specific events happen that marked our visits. We did all of the things tourists do, like take the tram from Central up the mountain on Hong Kong Island and saw the Big Buddha on Lantau Island. We saw the ruins of the cathedral in Macau. But Hong Kong and Macau are not about seeing the sights. They are about being Hong Kong and Macau, two legendary places that are exotic because so many aspects of them seem so familiar but out of place.
- *Interests beat ideology almost every time.* Twenty years ago, no one could have imagined China owning a financial haven and a gambling haven. Many wealthy Chinese residents of Hong Kong and Macau obtained citizenship in Canada and elsewhere before the colonies were handed over; they could not imagine China would fulfill its promises to leave the two places pretty much alone. Yet that is what China did and also encouraged casino investments. Ideological purity can be cumbersome and destructive, as China discovered during the first 30 years of

Communist rule. It can be inconvenient, as is the case with U.S. relations with Saudi Arabia. The U.S. government ignores the human rights violations in Saudi for economic and security reasons but has no trouble telling China to stop the same human rights violations because China is a rival.

Viney had many business meetings in Korea with company people, as well as other company professionals. Many of his experiences echoed those he had encountered in other parts of East Asia:

- Business cards and title are important; cards are given with both hands.
- Punctuality is expected, but my Korean contacts could cancel meetings.
- Personal relationships mean more than contracts.
- While title and seniority are important, decision-making involves the team, not an individual.
- Criticism is viewed as shaming someone, so I always gave any feedback in private.

Korea offers one amusing difference. Everywhere else in the world, finding two people in a company with the same surname is unusual unless it is a family business. In Korea, Kim and Park are incredibly common surnames. Every company has many Kims and Parks. It is unlikely any of the Kims will be related, or any of the Parks. Knowing a person's full name is essential. Korea has many interesting cultural and social features like this.

North–South enmity is known to all. Although a ceasefire was signed in 1953, the war has never ended officially. It is evident in all social discussions. Another major topic relates to Japan's occupation of Korea from 1895 to 1945. Japan forced thousands of Korean women to become prostitutes during the Second World War, moving many of them to Japan to be "comfort women" for Japanese soldiers. Japan is the most hated country by Koreans, and we could sense that talking to many Koreans. Although the Japanese government has provided some compensation, Koreans are still waiting for an apology for this barbaric action.

We visited the DMZ (Demilitarized Zone), easily the most electrifying experience of our visit to South Korea. This was a great trip for Kumud and me. A North Korean defector in 1978 revealed tunnels had been dug by North Korea to attack South Korea. Four tunnels were found. The tunnels could let 30,000 soldiers an hour into South Korea. We went inside the Third Tunnel of Northern Aggression located near Panmunjom. This tunnel is a popular tourist stop when visiting the DMZ from Seoul. We recall having to sign a declaration before going to the DMZ: "The visit to the DMZ-Joint Security Area at Panmunjom will entail the entrance into a hostile area and the possibility of injury or death as a direct result of enemy action." Scary enough, right? In the tunnel, we were technically on the north side of the border. To top it off, a stretch of about 200 yards was narrow enough for only one person. Viney is afraid of enclosed spaces and refused to go into that section. We had already had enough adventure.

Once in Korea, Viney was asked by one of his colleagues about his blood type. He said it is B positive. The colleague immediately started telling Viney about his personality based on blood type. In fact, he was damn accurate. We had never heard of such a thing, but Koreans believe blood type determines personality. Interesting how cultures find their own peculiarities. Viney was in the office signing a document with red ink. He was stopped by a colleague, who explained that red is a sign of death. Using red ink meant either Viney wished the death of the person who was going to receive the document or that person will die soon. Out of caution, Viney just didn't take red pens to Korea after that incident. Also, the number four scares Koreans. In Korean and Chinese, the word "four" is pronounced like the word "death." Buildings skip from the third to the fifth floor the way some Western buildings don't have a thirteenth floor. Most interestingly, Koreans count age from 1 not 0. The day the baby is born, he or she is considered to be one year old. As far as I can discover, Korea is the only country that does this.

Seoul is in the northwest of South Korea. The next largest city, Busan, is on the south coast. Our three-hour train ride from Seoul to Busan was enlightening. We saw many young Korean couples in identical T-shirts. We discovered this shows their deep love for each other, an example of how expressive Koreans can be about their relationships. Also, the train conductor bowed each time he passed in the compartment. We remembered a similar experience on Japanese trains as well. Korea is well known for having followed on Japan's heels building a strong industrial sector that includes automobiles, tires, electronics, and appliances. Samsung basically runs South Korea. Viney was told more than 20 percent of their GDP was influenced by Samsung. Samsung was an Accenture client.

Whenever we went for food, kimchi was served to us as one of the first items. Kimchi is a combination of vegetables and spices fermented underground for months, like a spicy, red salad. Typically, the vegetable is cabbage, which is the kind available in U.S. grocery stores. However, there are a wide range of vegetables used in Korea. On the subject of special foods, just as horse is a delicacy in Japan, dog is in Korea, available even on street sides. As for beverages, drinking is a way of life almost. We were given drinks everywhere. We even saw drunken Koreans who had passed out on sides of the streets. We had to wonder whether public intoxication was against the law, as it is in Western countries.

Ninth Interlude:
Australia and New Zealand (2011-13)

"Not all those who wander are lost."
J. R. R. Tolkien

Viney relates some of the pitfalls of travelling without properly checking rules and customs: During my first visit to Sydney at the beginning of 2011, I reached Singapore airport to board the Singapore Air flight to Sydney. I was surprised to learn that a visa was needed to go to Australia. I had assumed a U.S. passport holder did not need a visa to go to a friendly, Commonwealth country. Though there was little time to board the plane, the Singapore Airline customer service representative was able to get an e-visitor visa online in a few minutes for a price. The process was fairly simple.

During the same trip, by oversight, there were two apples in my hand luggage when we landed in Sydney. I had planned to eat them during the flight but could not and forgot to declare them. A detective dog sniffed my luggage and found the apples. The customs officials told me the punishment for bringing agricultural products is severe. One can be fined between A$180-$360 on the spot or one could be prosecuted, fined more than A$66,000, and risk 10 years in jail plus a criminal record, especially for items with biosecurity risk. I was told there were signs all over warning visitors of the ban on bringing any food items whatsoever into Australia. I was, however, excused by a generous officer since this was his first visit to Australia. It was a big lesson for me to follow the customs rules diligently and to pay attention to signage after deplaning in a country. Assumptions, ignorance, lack of attention: they will trip up travelers all of the time.

One big assumption we make or problem we forget is that English comes in many flavors. I was talking about Varun moving to a start-up. Someone asked what a start-up was. Perhaps the term has become better known, but it was surprising because Australian culture is similar to U.S. culture. Australia shares a common bond on many fronts with the U.S., not just in language. Naturally, there are bound to be some differences. The Australian accent is one; it is unique and sometimes difficult to understand. However, younger employees seem to be picking up an American accent and adopting it. Australians are more relaxed and casual, while Americans are more patriotic (flags flying in our front yards are a common sight) and more religious. Also, except in restaurants where you might tip if there is exceptional service, tips are not expected.

Australia has less than 10 percent of the U.S. population (22M vs 320M). The much smaller population and higher overall wages account for Australia having a narrower social divide compared to the U.S. Family welfare policies are very liberal, e.g. maternity and paternity leave is very generous: nine months for the new mother and three months for the new father. It isn't as good as Scandinavia, but much, much better than the U.S.

In dealings with many Australian friends, I found that they do not get impressed with you very easily; even if you impress them somehow, they will not admit it or show it. I rarely heard compliments from an Australian boss I had; he only showed his pleasure with my work through the annual evaluation. No one ever says, "Good job." Perhaps one reason we think Australian culture seemed similar is that so many aspects of it have been made known in the U.S. It was normal to say, "G'day" to all any time of the day.

On the business front where my dealings were frequent, business suits, punctuality, maintaining eye contact, and directness were all expected and encouraged. The easiest way to break the ice was to bring up cricket. Australians are crazy about cricket, and it provides a great informal start to a meeting. Since cricket also is a part of Indian culture, the discussion would set a tone of mutual interest.

Kumud, of course, made her way to Oz with me. We were able to see all the key tourist places in and around Sydney: the Opera House, Bondi Beach, Harbour Bridge, Darling Harbour, Manly Beach, Sydney Towers, Museum of Sydney, and the Blue Mountains. Australia is another of those countries, though, where seeing a part of it hardly tells the story. The country has an interesting parallel to Canada. A huge part of Canada's population lives within 50 miles or so of the border with the U.S. In Australia, a huge part of the population lives within 50 miles of the ocean.

Aside from Canada, Australia is the closest country culturally to the U.S. from many angles, but there are still many differences. Most of those differences relate to being sensitive while dealing with people. Australians are direct. At times, they seem arrogant or at least less friendly and more formal in common situations in which one would expect a more relaxed atmosphere. This seems to contradict the perception of Aussies as being laid back. However, as you build friendships, they get more comfortable.

New Zealanders are also called Kiwis, named for the indigenous, plain, ground-dwelling bird, not for the fruit (which are actually Chinese gooseberries, but kiwi is apparently more marketable). We had two separate trips to New Zealand: one to South Island to see Christchurch and Queenstown and the other to North Island to visit Auckland, the largest city. We were told class structure was more or less absent in New Zealand; wealth and social status are not important to Kiwis. The country is a "welfare state" that provides housing and healthcare free of charge to those who can't afford those necessities. Kiwis are very warm, courteous, and friendly people. When we went to Christchurch, the scars of their biggest earthquake were all over the city, but the spirits of the people were very upbeat.

One incident amply proves how amazing the people are. We were traveling by local bus in Christchurch and asked for directions to our destination from two bus drivers on two different routes. They were extra courteous, took a piece of paper, drew maps and took several minutes to explain in detail how to reach where we wanted to go after we got down. They even made many passengers wait to board the bus while explaining fully how to reach our destination. We observed a similar experience on another bus for other tourists in similar situations as ours. The only other place we can say this behavior is typical is Japan.

Our conducted bus journey from Christchurch to Queenstown took seven hours. We think it has been the best ride we have ever taken in our lives so far. Each sight was heavenly, natural beauty. After seeing hundreds of sheep grazing, the mountains and lakes began to appear. Every vista could be used to create a beautiful painting. It is no wonder many filmmakers go to EnZed to make use of the picturesque backdrops.

During our trip to Auckland with family from Seattle, we had a conducted tour to Rotorua and Canterbury to see Māori culture in action. Māori people make up 14 percent of the country's population and are the indigenous people of New Zealand. They arrived more than 1000 years ago from their Polynesian homeland of Hawaii. We had the good fortune to see Māori live performances, Māori speeches and singing, carved meeting houses, greeting them with the traditional pressing of noses, and enjoying a wonderful dinner cooked in earthen ovens. They place great value on hospitality and will spontaneously launch into speech and song. Everyone was asked to sing songs from their native lands. We sang an Indian song. Others sang Scandinavian, Polish, and French songs. It was a great experience getting to know their culture. Kiwis are environmentally concerned, an attitude towards the environment influenced by the viewpoint of the indigenous population, which believes that all things have a "mauri" or a life force.

On the business side, appointments are necessary for meetings but can be easily scheduled and happen on time. Meetings were relaxed but serious with eye contact as important as it was in Australia. Kiwis appreciate honesty and directness in business dealings. The negotiating process is serious, with realistic figures put on the table. It is definitely not a bargaining culture. In a souvenir shop, we tried to negotiate the price of some T-shirts. Our effort not only was not appreciated, the facial expression looked like "What the hell are you doing?"

New Zealand and Australia have open borders. Citizens can live and work in either country. One of Viney's university friends settled in NZ but has since moved to Australia and is working there now. Both countries share an interest in certain sports, like cricket and rugby brought by the British. Australians have higher incomes, but also a higher cost of living. Although we only saw a small part of Australia, we saw much of New Zealand. It is one of the greatest countries for natural, virgin beauty. Life is not all about achieving glory or other rewards. People enjoy what they have. While Aussies sometimes seemed impenetrable, the humility and friendliness of Kiwis give visitors memorable interactions.

Tenth Interlude:
Southeast Asia (2011-13)

*"Avoiding danger is no safer in the long run
than outright exposure.
Life is either a daring adventure or nothing."*
Helen Keller

A strong Buddhist culture predominates in Thailand, Indonesia, Malaysia, Vietnam, Cambodia, China, Hong Kong, Japan, South Korea, Singapore, and Sri Lanka. This culture produces many commonalities in the business and personal behavior in these countries. At times, passive aggression in the form of delaying decisions is one of the outcomes. In Vietnam, the U.S. is still not liked, and some Muslims in the region oppose U.S. policies. Be prepared. Shame in the form of acting so someone "loses face" must be avoided in most Asia-Pacific countries, particularly in Chinese, Malay, Indian, Korean, and Japanese cultures. Indeed, personal relationships are critical and paramount before business relationships are built, so the last thing any visitor wants to do is embarrass a member of his or another's team. Also, hierarchical structure is observed in businesses, as well as in families.

We mentioned the importance of business cards in discussing East Asian countries. It is necessary to fully grasp the importance attached to their use in Southeast Asia as well. A business card shows one's title and stature in the business, not to mention providing one's name for future reference. Given the face-to-face relationship-building necessary for success, a business card is almost like a little biography of the most important points about someone you need to get to know. Usually, cards have English on one side and the national language on the other side. Some people from the U.S. who make frequent visits to one or two countries will do the same. Cards are given and accepted with both hands. Cards should be treated with honor, so it is important not to write on them.

Gift giving also helps to support personal relationships, but they should be commensurate with the culture. One would never give

182

liquor or pork as a gift in Malaysia or Indonesia since these items cannot be consumed by faithful Muslims. Of course, flowers are universally acceptable when visiting any home. Our observations regarding Southeast Asian countries are similar to gift giving. Some practices are common throughout the region. Others are highly specific to one country. While repetitiveness is unavoidable, it is needed in order to put the specifics into context.

We made many trips to Thailand from 2011 to 2013. Viney had visited Bangkok in 1987 from Saudi Arabia. The country is overwhelmingly Buddhist – 95 percent of the population – and this is reflected in how calm and friendly people are, at least with foreigners (*farangs*). Thailand has been going through some difficult times politically due to the competition between a political party run by a billionaire that tries to represent the poor and rural residents and a party run by wealthy and middle class people who don't want a welfare state. The glue holding everything together is King Bhumibol Adulyadej, who has ruled since 1946, when he was just 19 years old. The royal family is held in high esteem. Thailand still retains a *lèse–majesté* law that makes it a criminal offense to criticize the king or royal family, but it has only been invoked once, in the 1950s against government ministers as grounds for their dismissal.

A visit to the Grand Palace along the Chao Praya River is a highlight of any visit to Bangkok. Actually, we loved all the tourist attractions: the Temple of the Golden Buddha, Patpong night market, Chinatown, the flower market, and countless more. The floating market was a great experience for us – just two hours' drive from Bangkok. The colorfully clad merchants at these lively markets paddle along narrow canals, selling all sorts of items. Thailand truly is one of the most fascinating countries on earth. Additionally, many things are inexpensive. We got hooked on Thai foot and shoulder massages, unimaginably relaxing and dirt cheap at $5 for 60 minutes. However, one of the ways to ensure things cost less is to make use of your bargaining skills.

We also flew to Phuket, an island off the west coast of Thailand. Phuket was the first resort area in the country outside greater Bangkok and has many attractions like Patong Beach, the Big

Buddha, Soi Bangla (a "sin city" for lonely men), and much more. Entertainment gives visitors things to do in the evening. We strongly recommend two not-to-miss shows:

- The Phuket FantaSea show in Kamala Beach was inspired by Thailand's rich culture. The presentation showcases ancient Thai traditions, with special effects and scores of large elephants in action. We were mesmerized.
- For something completely different, Phuket Simon Ladyboy Show claims to be the biggest transvestite cabaret show in the world, performed by the famous "ladyboys." We were in awe seeing their perfect figures, stunning costumes, and professional theatrical performances in melodious women voices.

Unfortunately, tourists must beware of scams, particularly false tourist agents and guides. The Marriott where we stayed in Bangkok is across the river from most of the tourist sites. Although one has to take a ferry, the view across to the gilded roofs is extraordinary. Kumud was approached by a guy dressed in a Marriott uniform. He told her the Palace was closed that day, so he would take her to a shopping mall. A man in palace guard uniform also said the Palace was closed. She walked down a bit farther and saw tourists all over in the palace grounds. On another occasion, we were offered an exclusive ferry ride back to the Marriott for 1,500 baht, when the usual price is only 30 baht. The higher price warranted a river cruise through the city, not just crossing from one bank to the other.

Imitation luxury goods must make up a big part of the Bangkok economy. They are everywhere. Sometimes to avoid prosecution, the makers make a small change to the brand name, like Bolex instead of Rolex. Viney bought a "Rolex" watch for $10 that worked very well and convinced friends he had the real deal. Needless to say, if someone is willing to cheat selling rip-offs, he is probably willing to cheat foreign customers as well. One of our friends chose a purse that the vendor showed to her. He went to a back room and returned with a box and told her not to open the box in the market. When she got back to her hotel room and opened the box, she found a junky purse. It was absolutely a scam. The problem is that Thai people are genuinely friendly, so some crooks take advantage of this and act just as friendly, not indicating at all that they are scamming you. The question is whether to be suspicious of everyone's motives and thereby rude to the sincere who make a visit so pleasant or trust there are bad apples in every barrel and thereby accept your visit will be overall enjoyable, even if there are one or two unsavory exchanges.

Overall, Viney's experience in Thai business meetings was very positive. Thai companies operate like many others in the region. Suit and tie are *de rigueur*. Business cards are treated the same as elsewhere. Punctuality means that the meeting both starts on time and ends on time. Patience is essential since decision making is slow. And unfortunately, yes does not always mean yes. Overall, our Thai experiences were positive, and we found the people quite friendly.

Kumud and I visited Jakarta and Bali on two different trips. Indonesia must be the most fascinating country that hardly anyone knows anything about. It is the world's fourth most populous nation and largest Muslim nation, with two-to-three hundred ethnic groups living among 17,500 islands. The capital, Jakarta, does not offer much to see and explore except some historical places like the national monument, national gallery, etc. However, it is probably the only place in the country where a visitor can see people from the various ethnic groups without having to hop around the islands.

Bali is special because the culture is based on Hindu and Buddhist traditions. Most shopping places in Bali assume tourists are rich and try to make easy money, something that also happened with us in Jakarta. We learned it is best to take a local friend with you for shopping. You will get a better deal and not be scammed. Bali has many interesting sites. We stayed in the Kuta area but saw most of the historical and cultural places especially temples. Aside from the excellent beaches, Bali is a place to relax with yoga, meditation, massages, and spas. Though there had been bomb blasts in 2002 and 2005, the tourist inflow has not decreased, especially from the Western countries. Most youth from Western countries rent two-wheelers to zip around the island.

I met with many executives of other companies on visits to Indonesia. Business suits were the norm, a feature throughout

Southeast and East Asia that was interesting because it was a clearly deliberate effort to imitate Westerners and forsake local dress. Many a time, I had a different interpretation of meetings than his colleagues. I have been used to directness, not needing to figure out whether someone meant what I said. Inference was important in trying to understand what was being said. However, no matter how great the dispute might be, Indonesians prefer no confrontations or arguments. I never participated in a loud meeting. This partly arises from the emphasis on personal relationships over company relationships; no one will want to argue with a friend. As is rampant in the region, decision making is slow and an outsider must show patience. Sometimes discussions are dragged out simply because they just don't want to say no.

Kumud and I reached Kuala Lumpur airport in Malaysia during the second week of May 2011, a week after Osama bin Laden was killed by U.S. troops. We took a cab from the airport and were on our way to the hotel. The driver became friendly with us and started talking about politics. He thought we were Indian nationals. When we told him we were U.S. nationals, he suddenly became angry, saying the U.S. is evil. They killed Osama, and that was not right. Kumud and I immediately realized we were in a Muslim country and not everybody in the Muslim world looked on Osama bin Laden as a terrorist. That was a lesson for us to limit our conversations to general topics. This was not the first time we saw that U.S. nationals are not particularly welcome in a country due to local perceptions of global affairs. So we just stopped saying we were from the U.S. and instead pretended to be Indian nationals. Of course, Kumud apparently could pretend to be almost any nationality.

From centuries of trade and interaction, three major groups reside in Malaysia: Malays who are mostly Muslims, Indians who are mostly Hindus and Sikhs, and Chinese who are mostly Buddhists. However, since Malays are the majority, the country has been declared a Muslim state. Islam dictates customs, dress, and gender relationships. Men wear a suit and a tie and women dress as formally, along with a head scarf. Meetings on Fridays are avoided since it is the holy day of the week. However, most of the rules, like the use of business cards, are the same as in many other countries.

Personal relationships are just as critical, decision making is just as slow, hierarchy is just as important, and shame is just as weighty. The two aspects that are different are the relaxed attitude about punctuality and the universal use of given names of people in meetings rather than surnames.

We went to Manila, capital of the Philippines, during the first to second week of February 2013. That was when Chinese New year is celebrated. This is a major festival in most of Southeast Asia due to the long history of Chinese merchants forming settlements to assist their trading activities. We still recall it was February 10, 2013. The Sheraton had a huge ceremony and party for all the hotel guests, as well as paying participants from the city. The unveiling of the 2013 animal was done at midnight in a glittering ceremony outside the hotel. The animal for 2013 was the snake. We made friends with many local Chinese settled in Manila.

We hired an exclusive tour guide for us in Manila. Whenever this is within a traveler's budget and reputable businesses offer it, this is absolutely the best way to spend a day getting to know a city and see the major sights. Oftentimes, the prices are quite reasonable. The cars are comfortable or you just don't go. The guide/driver is friendly and knowledgeable not just about the city, but also the culture, giving tourists personal insights they could never get on their own or with a group. Most are so good that if you don't have enough cash for a generous tip at the end of the day, you will find yourself asking the guide to take you to an ATM as the last stop. Moreover, if done on the first day of a multi-day visit, one then knows enough about the city to feel more confident going around and has spied some unique places to visit or discovered others that deserve a longer look.

Before starting the trip, our guide gave us some Do's and Don'ts. One of them was to take care of our wallets and valuables, as pickpocketing was not uncommon. And then, he surprised us by saying that while Viney should be careful, Kumud need not worry about it. He thought Kumud was Filipino. As we have hinted, Kumud's features have been a big asset for us where people have mistaken her to be a wide range of nationalities. What nationality locals think she is might be a running joke in the family, but the fact remains we are proud she blends in wherever she goes as a natural part of the population. In reality, she signifies and defines us as a global family.

Most Filipinos speak English and due to American influence follow many of the Western rules when it comes to business. However, while some meetings in the U.S. can get heated, raising one's voice in Manila is suicidal. Filipinos follow Gandhi's philosophy in business and personal life, using a passive way to deal with most things. The same rules for business cards apply as in most of Asia. Filipinos have many names, including nicknames, so it is always better to ask them how they would like to be addressed than make a mistake. Yes does not always mean yes, and no does not always mean no. The goal seems to remain ambiguous during a slow decision-making process.

We went to Vietnam in 2012. Before going, we were told by our friends who had recently visited Vietnam to beware of drivers out to fleece foreigners. They told us to fix the price of the ride in advance with the driver instead of relying on the taxi meter. It seems most of the meters are corrupted. We still made this mistake on a mile trip to the hotel that ended up being five times as much as it should have been.

It amazed us that the immigration officials at Ho Chi Minh City airport expected bribes from us on entry as well as exit. Apparently, they have become used to getting some cash from foreigners. The trick is to put money in your passport before handing it to border official. We decided not to give in to extortion, which resulted in having a tough time with the officials. However, they could not refuse our entry since we had pre-arrival visas that are a pre-requisite for entry to Vietnam.

Wherever we went in Vietnam, the U.S. was not a preferred nation. There is a museum showing atrocities of U.S. troops during the Vietnam War. While the historical record shows that U.S. troops crossed the line at times, we were appalled to see the Vietnamese attitude towards the U.S. remaining so hostile. Most citizens think the U.S. was unnecessarily involved in the war and created a lot of problems for the common man and caused a lot of destruction. When faced with such strong perspectives, we always have found it best to be silent and reflect on how much those opinions are grounded in truth and reason and how much on propaganda and anger.

I was sitting with one of the executives of a company over a business dinner, and the conversation ran something like this over American involvement in Vietnam War:

Vietnamese Executive: "The past is past. We can't change it. Now we business people think you to be a friend rather than an enemy." And suddenly he looked straight into my eyes and said, "Vietnamese culture is influenced by Buddhism and teaches forgiveness. As long as you agree you made mistakes and regret making them, we have no reason to hate you."

This sentiment was apparent within much of the business community, but the general public as yet cannot forget or forgive.

Vietnam is clearly the moped capital of the world. It was interesting to see hundreds of mopeds stopped at red lights. Each time our car stopped at a red light, Kumud and I tried to count how many mopeds came up and stopped also. We found it was impossible to count; sometimes there were close to one thousand, just overwhelming swarms. We stopped counting afterwards and accepted the Vietnamese as kings of the moped world. One of the great things about traveling as a couple is to latch onto these kinds of silly diversions that are pointless but amusing in the moment.

Despite remaining a communist country, business etiquette follows the same concepts of hierarchy, shame, personal relationships, and group decision making common in that part of the world. While that may be resoundingly redundant, it is actually a very profound comment on the interplay of traditional cultural norms and modern ideological frameworks. Revolutions can sweep away political and economic structures like a tsunami, but the new structures are still built on the same ground.

We went to Phnom Penh, the capital of Cambodia by bus from Ho Chi Minh City (Saigon) in Vietnam. The journey was very interesting. The whole bus ride of 180 miles took around 8 hours. The pace was not slow; getting across the border was. The driver of the bus collected passports from everybody to obtain visas at the Cambodian border. The process is very chaotic. All of the passengers were ushered into a hall where passengers from various other buses were also waiting. The immigration official called the names one by one for visa processing. There was no apparent order. It took more than two hours to get through the immigration. A border officer just looked at the passport and looked at the person. It seemed they expected bribes, but we didn't do it. Although we feared our passports might get lost, no harm was done.

On our way to Phnom Penh, the bus crossed a river by ferry. The ferry was very old and had many buses and trucks on it. We feared, what if the old ferry sinks? Of course, it didn't. We had come a long way from being awestruck at vehicles going onto the ferry at Dover on our way to Paris years before. We were even further removed from the memories stirred by the next sight. The Cambodian side had mango trees all through the route, and they were loaded with ripe mangoes. Viney was reminded of his childhood and how his family used to go every week to the mango gardens of students' families to feast on the juicy mangoes.

We were surprised to see the strong influence of Hindu culture in Cambodia. The most famous example is Angkor Wat (meaning temple city), a 500-acre monument richly decorated with statues and bas reliefs. The largest Hindu temple dedicated to Vishnu was built around 1150 CE. The complex has been named a UNESCO World Heritage Site.

The tuk-tuk is the most pleasant and most breezy transport in Phnom Penh. They look a bit like three-wheeled golf carts but are driven like they are mopeds. We hired one for $20 per day. The going rate was $2 per hour. Though we were coached to negotiate, we did not because it was fairly cheap anyway. The advantage is that the tuk-tuk driver will wait for you at every site, no matter how long you take. Most of the tuk-tuk drivers are knowledgeable about the places to visit and know the short cuts also. We saw all the historical places, including the royal palace, independence monument, national museum of arts, Tuol Sleng Museum (an example of Khmer Rouge atrocities), and the lively central market.

We flew back from Phnom Penh to Ho Chi Minh City. Once again, the immigration officials were clearly expecting a tip from us. This problem is common because many foreigners go along with it. We were told many people slip a US$10 bill or more in their passport. It is sad such a practice by government officials is happening. We are guessing they were making $300-$400 per day from this illegal activity. How sad? Our not giving the tip gave us pitiable customer services, but that is an easier price to pay than participating in graft. Interestingly, when we left the country, we went through Phnom Penh again as transit passengers and saw a parked plane at the airport with huge lettering, United States of America, inscribed on the fuselage. On enquiry, we were told Hilary Clinton, then Secretary of State, was visiting the region at that time.

Business customs followed the pattern of other countries in the region. Reverence for a hierarchical culture meant respect to the most senior person. Meetings do not stick to any schedule. They just go on. Personal relationships trump company relationships, and decision making never seems to reach the point where an actual decision will be made. Like Thailand, a large part of the population is Buddhist, but Cambodians seem to include their belief in Karma (as you sow, so shall you reap) in business matters.

We visited Sri Lanka in 2012 and stayed mainly in Colombo. We hired a driver to show us around Colombo. He was jovial and friendly but kept on pestering us to go shopping. In spite of our repeatedly saying no, he finally took us to a garment shop where silk items were for sale. We bought a few items to be polite. Later, we were told by our hotel staff that all drivers in Sri Lanka are underpaid and get hefty commissions for taking customers to different shopping places, especially jewelry shops. Whenever possible, it is best to avoid any shopping arranged through tours and hired drivers unless the products are something you truly want. Otherwise, just tell the driver his tip will depend on how few shops he takes you to. That ought to take care of the problem!

Kumud and I decided to go to Kandy and took a train from Colombo, a ride of two and a half hours. The train system in Sri Lanka is still primitive. The trains, as well as stations, are far from state of the art. Although we had the air-conditioned coach, it felt like we were getting suffocated. Kandy is renowned because Sinhalese culture (the majority ethnic group) is so visibly on display there, and most importantly, the Temple of the Tooth (the Buddha's tooth) is there. It is important enough to be a UNESCO World Heritage Site. On our way back in the evening, Kumud caught a bad virus on the train. She had a high temperature for the next few days that concerned us. Back in Colombo, we looked for a doctor but did not find the right one. Kumud had to travel back to Singapore running a fever. It was an unforeseeable dampener for this otherwise enjoyable, educational trip. Given how rarely our travels have been interrupted by any surprise, we were just grateful the virus was not worse.

Our biggest regret is not to have gone to explore the country by safari, go on road trips, and visit the seashores due to Kumud's sickness. We will definitely go back one day.

As we mentioned at the beginning of this section, the countries of this region have many similarities. In business situations, it is easy enough to learn from the experience in one country and apply those lessons to the next. We found that the same was true from the tourist viewpoint as well.

- *Respect and learn from the cultural aspects of a country.* Saying anything against the King or Queen of Thailand is a punishable crime. Even if, as a visitor, one does not know this, why would you be disrespectful of any part of a country's culture while there? The wonderful thing about the need to build personal relationships in a business context is that you are less likely to do offensive things like shame someone openly. The people with whom you have relationships are going to teach you how to navigate their culture. Buddhist teachings are clearly evident in the attitudes of people; they are calm, friendly, believing in destiny. The opportunity is there to learn how they integrate these positive features into their lives. The opportunity also is there to take advantage of the way people rejuvenate, like through meditation or massages.
- *Everything is negotiable, and it is better to walk away than be scammed.* It is interesting how the business world considers give and take to reach agreement as natural, but Westerners are so unused to bargaining in daily activities and are so used to paying the prices they see, they don't bargain in countries where bargaining is expected. This includes taxi fares sometimes and other things one might never expect are negotiable. The

principle of negotiation is to start almost absurdly low. Ignore people who hound you or try to convince you to do things their way. Scammers and drivers will say anything to get you to a store where they will get a commission for taking tourists. Corruption is not the monopoly of any country or any profession. And always, always make certain that what you get is what you purchased.

- *English is a blessing and a curse.* We found that it is critical to have an English speaking tourist guide. One guide in Sri Lanka did not speak English, and we missed out on some finer details of many tourist spots. On the other hand, being clearly from the U.S. or a Western country is not always helpful. The price of the items will go up dramatically. As the saying goes, "For you, special price." U.S. nationals must be prepared for some bashing from some quarters. Best to see this as an unavoidable resentment against the one global power rather than an insult. A tourist cannot adopt the perspective a resident has of the tourist's country; it is pointless to argue over distinct viewpoints that will never line up.

- *Multiculturalism works reasonably well.* One mark of an advanced society is its ability to protect minorities. Malaysia has the most obvious division between the majority Malays and minority Indians and Chinese, but everyone works together. Indonesia has a good balance between majority Muslims and minority Hindus in Bali, but also among the many ethnic groups. Minorities in Thailand and the Philippines live in border areas and so are much less visible. However, divisions in those countries seem to be over political policies rather than communal issues.

- *Safety is critical, and one needs to stay vigilant.* No matter how many times one falls prey to scams, you can still fall prey to another. It is just too difficult to keep one's guard up all the time, particularly when one doesn't speak the local language and are unfamiliar with where things are. Safety is your personal responsibility. However, nothing can be gained by dwelling on bad experiences since they will ruin the good memories of a trip.

If We Had Taken the Road More Traveled

"I shall be telling this with a sigh
Somewhere ages and ages hence:
Two roads diverged in a wood, and I—
I took the one less traveled by,
And that has made all the difference."
Robert Frost

Living involves making millions of choices. Almost all of the decisions we make are trivial, demand little thought, and generate minute consequences. We do not take action worrying if what we decide will somehow snowball into a huge change in our destiny or that of anyone else. We do not use the Butterfly Effect of chaos theory—the notion that if a butterfly flaps its wings a certain way, a hurricane will develop a few weeks later—to choose whether to take the stairs or the elevator. We decide and decide and decide with little or no conscious effort.

Living, however, sometimes brings us to a fork in the road. We must choose a path. There is nothing trivial about the decision. We spend our time carefully thinking about each option. The consequences will have a great impact on our lives, and probably the lives of our family members. Part of our thought processes involves trying to discern what those consequences will be if we take one path instead of the other. We want to forecast the future like a meteorologist using the best rational methods available. We sometimes seek the services of psychics and astrologers, putting our trust (and money) in the hands of people we hope will provide us with direction. We want to make the "right" decision, not just because it is better, but also because we don't want to look back in the future at a mistake.

Some historians speculate about how important individual events have been to the flow of history by proposing counterfactuals, alternative events to replace the one being studied. They want to test the strength of the event as a cause of future events. An entire genre of fiction, alternative history, has developed around the idea of describing what happens if an actual historical event didn't happen or happened differently. Individuals reflecting on the course of their lives engage in a similar process. The difference is that individuals know what the options had been. The counterfactual is the path not taken. Extrapolating from a decision to determine what would have happened if we chose differently would be like writing an alternative history of our own lives. The problem for too many people is that they look back at major choices and write a happier history for themselves if they had only made the "right" decision instead of the one they did. They look at their "bad" decisions and create a pile of regrets that prevents them from seeing the good decisions they have made or the possibilities in the present.

Looking back on more than six decades of our mortal lives, we see at least a dozen or more places where we faced a fork in the road or sometimes an intersection that gave us three options: left, right, or forward. As we have repeatedly mentioned, we routinely took the riskier path. Our goal was not to be adventurous. Indeed, sometimes the choice made us quite anxious because we were facing unknowns like moving to Canada or knowns that were not reassuring like moving to Iraq while Iraq was at war. We chose the riskier route primarily because it appeared to be the better opportunity, offered greater future opportunities, or coincided best with our goals at that time. But how different would this story have been if we had chosen the well-worn trail more often? What might have happened if we took the safe road?

Clearly, the earliest choices led us to crossroads we never would have encountered if we had chosen differently. The sooner we diverge from the path we actually took, the faster later options become almost impossible to occur. When we are making choices as teenagers and young adults, or even when our parents make choices that affect our early lives, all of the possibilities are spread out before us. However, every one of those choices narrows the probabilities of some future options and increases the probabilities of others.

We do indeed shape the future, but not so definitively that we can know with any certainty that choosing A will result in B. Several billion other people are making decisions, too. Some of their choices are going to shape our future. If the Lente family had never decided to go to Iraq, we would not have gone to Turkey with them. If we had still gone by ourselves, we likely would have been refused entry for not having visas. The fact we were traveling with a French family may have been the deciding factor in the border officials making an exception. The Lentes' decision to become expats in Iraq was them choosing which fork to take in their road; that decision appeared to us as luck when we tried to enter Turkey. We can never know what impact the choices of others will have on how our choices play out. That is not to say we should give up on making the best decisions for ourselves based on the information we have. We just need to recognize that what civilizations have called fate, luck, or fortune is the cumulative effect of unknowable factors, like the decisions of others, on our choices. We were literally fortunate. Fortune favored us time after time. Would that have been so if we had taken the well-traveled road more often?

Here are more counterfactuals to explore that question.

- What if Viney had been born to rich parents and not seen all of the hardships of childhood that provide valuable lessons? In this scenario, it is unlikely Viney's father would have been a school principal and been as dedicated to advancement through education. He would not have experienced village life and the many opportunities to appreciate the small things of life that have greater significance when one's routine is mundane. For example, the mango picnics are not only a fond memory, but also a reminder to share one's "harvest", whatever that might be. Additionally, Viney would not have had to work as hard to advance his career and discover the value of life-long self-improvement.
- What if Viney had not defied his parents' expectation he should become a naturopath? Viney already had worked hard to follow their desire that he become a doctor. Becoming a naturopath was just a back-up option. Certainly, he would have demonstrated filial devotion by entering the naturopathy program, but at the expense of feeling as though he was an "also-ran." Defying his parents' wish was the first risk he took, setting a precedent for decisions down the line. Fulfilling his parents' wish would have

set a far different precedent, one that elevated obedience to others over obedience to one's own heart.

- What if we had succumbed to Viney's father's wishes and not married? Literature is filled with stories of unrequited love, but the happy endings demanded by romance readers always bring the couple together in the end. We certainly gave him enough time to come around to the idea that Kumud was exactly the kind of bride he would have chosen for Viney. He eventually acknowledged this long after we were married. At the time, he was stubbornly sticking to the tradition he knew, which was that parents arrange marriages for their offspring. Had we not married, once again we would have spurned risk for the safe path. Eventually married to others, it is doubtful either one of us would have ever taken the risk to leave India.

- What if we had not left our comfort zone and a cozy government job to venture out of India to war-torn Iraq? Two things prompted us to go: Viney's oldest brother Krishan being in Iraq and able to look for a position for Viney, and Viney's disappointment about being moved about by the Agriculture Department, particularly sending him from the far more interesting position in Shillong to the Potato Institute in Simla. If we had seriously moved to Simla, we would have been avoiding risk. The government job was secure and up to that point beneficial and interesting. We had enjoyed being posted to Hyderabad and Shillong. Simla would not have been the summer capital of the British Raj if it didn't have its own charms. We were better off than many Indians. But staying in India with the Agriculture Department and hoping to enter the IAS left our destinies in the hands of others. We may never have met and befriended many non-Indians and been introduced to their cultures. We may never have visited Europe that sowed the seeds of immigration to the Western world in our minds. We would have been accepting a narrow, uninteresting path that would have made us narrow and uninteresting as well.

- What if Kumud had put her foot down and not moved to the Middle East with Viney in the 1980s and stayed in India in her banking job? The fact is that hundreds of thousands of men from southern and southeastern Asia take jobs in the Middle East that do not allow them to move their families to be with them. They work to send money home and see their wives or parents during one short trip each year, their only vacation. Having already been separated while we were engaged, we knew it would be even more difficult since Viney was not going to be able to just hop on a plane every month like he hopped on trains from Hyderabad. This would have denied us years of experiences together. We would not have visited Kumud's sister in London, most likely. Viney might not have accepted the transfer to Saudi Arabia and instead been forced to return to India to look for a job. And it is less likely our son would have been conceived, and definitely unlikely we would have named him Saddam.

- What if we had not gone to London and Paris and discovered we liked Western culture and saw Indians treated as equals? While our experiences in Iraq opened our eyes to a variation on the underdevelopment we already knew from India, our visit to London and Paris, at Christmas no less, gave us an entirely new way of seeing the world. We saw plenty. We saw gaiety. We saw equality. We saw freedom. Had we not taken that trip, it would be as though we would have remained blind to some of the colors in the spectrum. Our friends in the Kingdom may still have convinced us to immigrate to Canada, but we would not have been as open to the idea of moving to a Western culture where we thought we would be treated as second-class colonials.

- What if the door of Canadian immigration had not opened for us through a chance encounter at a social dinner in Riyadh? So much can happen as a result of the smallest decisions, such as whether to attend a dinner party. We never know what the consequences will be of any action we take. As a result of our trip to London and Paris, we already had the idea to move to Europe. London was a likely candidate since Kumud's sister lived there and we had seen the lively Punjabi community. We were getting to the point where the restrictiveness of Saudi society was becoming less and less sufferable. However, we hadn't taken any action yet to leave. Had we not been tipped off about Canada, it is very unlikely moving to Canada would have been an option we would consider. That would mean the option to move to Chicago and the option to move to Singapore would have evaporated. Moreover, we would not have been prompted to take action to immigrate as soon as we did. In all probability, we eventually would have ended up in London, but we may have first gone back to India or waited until Viney was hired by a British company. Certainly, our children's lives would have been extremely different.

- What if Viney had not raised his hand in a Tenneco management meeting in Canada to lead ISO 9001 certification for the company? What if we had listened to the astrologer in Canada and not taken the U.S. assignment? Viney's action opened the door to the U.S. for us. Clearly, we were quite happy in Canada with good jobs, a pleasant house, and good schools for Varun and Megha. Aside from the shady used car salesman, the delinquents we had as tenants, and the bank robbery, our experiences had been uniformly positive. Indeed, we had wanted Kumud's mother to live with us permanently, expected that Viney's father would return given how fascinated he was with his visit, and were looking forward to Krishan and his family immigrating. Staying in Canada would not have been bad for us, and we would have felt settled a little earlier than we did. The idea of staying sounded good enough that we did consult the astrologer for guidance. However, if Viney had not volunteered and if we had taken the astrologer's advice, his career would have remained somewhat mundane absent some other opportunity from Tenneco. Viney would not have been actively involved in the globalizing economy. We would not have moved to Singapore and visited so many countries. Megha would have likely gone to a Canadian university and never met Vivek.

- What if Kumud had not agreed to move back to India in 1997 as an expatriate? If Viney had taken the assignment, the same issues of separation would have resulted as when Viney got the job in Iraq and permission to move his family. However, Kumud would not have felt the stresses of moving for the eighth time in eighteen years. Her health would not have weakened, requiring several years of rehabilitation back to full strength. Varun could have remained in his school. Kumud could have gone to Omaha and Phoenix to help Megha with her grief. Assuming Viney had completed the three years planned for the assignment, Tenneco would have planned a position for him in Chicago that was more suitable than the Y2K lead he was offered, and he likely would have stayed with Tenneco a bit longer at least. He would not have found the position at Accenture when he did and would not have enjoyed the benefits he obtained from joining that company.

- What if Kumud had not agreed to move to Singapore in 2010? The separation issue comes up again if Viney took the assignment anyway. Kumud and Viney would not have shared the many trips to fifteen countries that reinforced the humorous fact that wherever we went, people thought Kumud was anything but Indian: in China, someone congratulated Viney for marrying a Chinese woman, in Singapore a Burmese woman thought Kumud was also Burmese, in the U.S., people thought she was Mexican, in Europe, Spanish, etc. That anecdote underscores how much enjoyment we got from travel, enjoyment that we would have missed if Kumud did not want to move to Singapore. We also enjoyed spending time with each other, more time than most empty-nesters find to rekindle their relationship. Two words, carrot juice, demonstrate how important Singapore was to our relationship; our trips every evening to get fresh carrot juice provided us with a simple but deeply meaningful way to strengthen our bonds. Also in Singapore, the steady, warm climate relieved Kumud of arthritis pain. Her health was the exact opposite of what it had been like in Delhi in 1997-98.

- What if Viney had not gathered the courage to retire from Accenture in 2015? One of the great benefits of exploring one's spirituality is it becomes easier to see the choices we can make. The decisions we have made in our lives indicate we have known this innately all along. We have made choices that we can lay claim to as ours and not as choices someone else made for us. We have controlled our destinies through our actions. Sometimes, the choice is whether to end a relationship that has been of great significance to your personal development and has created numerous pleasant memories. Nothing has happened necessarily to sour the relationship. It just seems to be the time to end that chapter. These feelings began when we returned from Singapore. There were things we wanted to do that required more time than one has while working full time. Jobs, however trivial, involve so much of our time that not having one creates a kind of vertigo from having so much freedom. And one does not just leave a position; one leaves relationships with colleagues, spaces one has occupied, and reasons for getting started in the morning. It is one thing to look forward to retirement from a job. It is quite another to decide to retire from a career that has progressed upward consistently and been rewarding intellectually, personally, and financially. Viney could have stayed at Accenture and remained very happy with the work and the people. However, he would be gnawed at by tasks he had put off, like writing this book, until they shamed him into retiring. Better to make the choice rather than let someone else, even your subconscious, make the choice for you.

Looking back, the only damaging decision we made was returning to India in 1997. In some ways, that was one of the least risky decisions we made. We knew the country. We would be close to relatives. We were excited to be expats in our homeland. Viney's position was high profile. Megha could focus on her freshman year studies. Varun could continue his American curriculum and become more familiar with the land of his ancestors. The riskier choice seemed to be refusing the assignment and possibly being let go by Tenneco, or at least having Viney's loyalty to the company questioned.

Instead, we ignored Kumud's anxiety about leaving Megha alone in the U.S. We ignored Kumud's concern about moving for the eighth time in eighteen years. We ignored Kumud having to give up her job again. We ignored the fact that Viney would be traveling so frequently, thinking Kumud's mother living with us would be sufficient to keep her spirits up. We ignored the possibility that Megha might find herself in an emergency situation, a not that infrequent occurrence in the first year of college, without us to support her. We ended up learning we had made the wrong choice at the expense of Kumud's health.

How many of us take the risk of choosing the less-travelled road? How many of us create paths for ourselves that others may follow? The well-travelled road was once just as risky and unclear as today's less-travelled road. People have been using Watling Street in southern England as a thoroughfare for about 2500 years, but before then the Briton tribes just trudged along through meadows and forded rivers long and often enough to create a clear track through the vegetation and riverbanks that the Romans found and paved. The Oregon Trail didn't magically come into being; it was forged by scores of wagons creating ruts that can still be seen today. Someone has to take the less-travelled road, or it will become overgrown and disappear, no longer an option for people journeying through life.

We can say we have been lucky. We can say that we always chose what we thought was the best option for us. We can say we were guided by the idea that we did not want to have regrets later on. Just because we chose riskier options early in our adult lives did not have to preclude us from aging into being more risk averse. Besides, the well-travelled road poses risks or adventures, too. No one can escape tragedy or excitement. We believe that if life is going to be truly fulfilling, we must seize the opportunities that come our way. The road less travelled just has more opportunities waiting for us.

The Journey Continues (2016-)

"I see my path, but I don't know where it leads.
Not knowing where I'm going is what inspires me to travel it."
Rosalia de Castro

The title of this book is derived from a well-known aphorism created by a significant figure in history. Each chapter and interlude in this book begins with a quotation from obscure to famous people sharing their views about travel, discovery, or learning. The title, quotations, and chapters together describe the experiences, events, and encounters that explain the lessons we have drawn as we transformed from a Punjabi couple to two global citizens. Our own globalization has given us a balanced, multifaceted view of things

The debates regarding globalization focus almost exclusively on the web of interconnected corporations, financial institutions, and governments, the detrimental effects on one economy in favor of another, and the end of sustainable local productivity should world trade face a major crisis. It all sounds quite bad until someone realizes that globalization helps products remain available and affordable. What the discussion completely overlooks is the way in which a global economy increases the opportunities for individuals to learn the similarities and differences between populations and cultures. Individuals can discover they are connected to every other person in the world. Globalization opens doors to experiences that reduce ignorance, prejudice, and conflict.

Our species has been traveling for ages. A small, initial population in what is now Kenya or Ethiopia spread everywhere, including, eventually, Antarctica and, temporarily, the Moon. Homo sapiens began to settle in particular locations only with the introduction of agriculture. Soon, more and more people were tied to the land in order to have enough food for growing populations. Journeys to find new environments continued as populations grew too large for one area to sustain. Journeys to expel populations to seize resources and journeys of refugees to find homes appeared. However, individuals and small groups rarely undertook traveling farther than to the nearest market town. Aside from religious pilgrims, curious philosophers, and risk-taking traders, long distance travel was unthinkable except by the Norsemen around 1000 CE and Ming China 400 years later. Then Portugal and other European countries set about finding a way to reach the production centers of spices in order to cut out the Indian, Arab, and Venetian middlemen. Europeans found the Americas and the various peoples and polities of a New World. Whereas globalization had first meant the migration of humans to fill every environment on the planet, now globalization was the process of reconnecting those migrants with one another. Mercantilism, evangelism, colonization, industrialization, and capitalism created a dense web of transmission lines, with almost all of the messages originating in Europe and North America.

Radical innovations in transportation and communications technologies, combined with two horrific global wars, hastened the demise of isolation. A review of the contents of the National Geographic Society's magazine over the decades reveals a shift from reports on "exotic" cultures and locales to articles on the impact of politics and war, scientific breakthroughs, and the exploits of individual explorers pursuing unusual feats like walking across Africa near the equator. This does not mean that *National Geographic* readers have become fluent in world cultures; it means there are many fewer cultures that warrant an article that would duplicate information easily found on the Internet. Fewer edges and corners of the known world are left to explore.

Except that is not true for individuals like us. We have described at some length our experiences living in six countries. We have supplemented that with highlights of visits to twenty-nine other countries, two autonomous territories, and our accidental trip into an unrecognized state (the Turkish Republic of Northern Cyprus). Each step of the way, we have shared the lessons we derived from those experiences. Each step of the way has provided new lessons. How much more can we learn? What more do we need to do to reinforce our credentials as global citizens?

T. S. Eliot wrote, "The journey, not the arrival, matters." Our experience is not how many places we have visited. It is the visiting itself, the transit of time as we move through new spaces. While there may be few places on this planet left to be explored, there are scores of places left to be explored by us. The United Nations counts 195 sovereign states at present. That leaves us with 166 remaining, not to mention all of the autonomous territories and colonies like Greenland, the Cook Islands, several Caribbean islands, etc. We have been to just 15 percent of the independent countries in the world. And we haven't necessarily seen much of them. We saw pretty much all there is to see in Iraq and Saudi. It isn't that difficult to cover all of Singapore, Hong Kong, or Macao. However, we haven't been to the Maritime Provinces of Canada, northern England or southern France, all regions quite different than the sections of those countries we have visited.

Since Viney's retirement, we already have managed to visit Alaska and Hawaii in the U.S., plus revisit Singapore and India. Although the film started everyone referring to a "bucket list," that designation makes it sound like a race against death to accomplish what one wants. More helpful to us is the idea of living as though today is one's last while planning as though one will live forever. We recognize that after a certain age, mobility and fragility become increasingly difficult issues to overcome. All we can do is see what we can do before our bodies say, "Slow down" and then, "Stop." We believe if we make sure we see the things we want before 75, any further chapters in our odyssey after that will be serendipitous treasures.

The places we would like to see fall into three categories:

- Return visits to enjoy or explore further places that we found most interesting;
- Travels to places we have not been yet; and
- Itineraries that are provoked by the idea we just want to say, "We saw that."

In the first category, we have a return to Nepal to visit the mountaineers' base camps, an exploration of the far north of India that takes us to a different part of the Himalayas than Nepal, a journey to Tibet to see a far different side of China and another Buddhist culture, an extended trip back to New Zealand to see both

205

North and South Islands top to bottom and coast to coast, and a cruise around the Aegean Islands to link our visits to Athens and Cyprus.

The places we have never seen but definitely want to see are South Africa since that seems to be the best way to introduce oneself to Africa, Antarctica so we can say (after visiting Africa) that we have visited every continent and it's every explorer's dream to see the bottom of the world, Malta to see a different side to Mediterranean life, and islands in the Indian Ocean like the Maldives and Mauritius that are as famed as Tahiti, Fiji, and Hawaii for being far off bits of paradise.

The third group includes two ideas. We would like to visit Eastern Europe, perhaps by way of Danube and Baltic cruises. Since the Soviet bloc fell apart a quarter century ago, the countries in that region have reasserted their national cultures, but the remnants of one-party rule remain. The second idea is to see the Seven New Wonders of the World: Chitchen Itza, Christ the Redeemer, Taj Mahal, Machu Picchu, the Great Wall of China, Coliseum, and Petra. Or the Seven Wonders of the Modern World: Channel Tunnel, CN Tower, Empire State Building, Golden Gate Bridge, Itaipu Dam, Netherlands North Sea Protection Works, and Panama Canal. Or Seven Natural Wonders: Grand Canyon, The Great Barrier Reef, The Harbor at Rio de Janeiro, Mt. Everest, Northern Lights, Paricutin Volcano, and Victoria Falls. Some of the third group places we already have seen, but there are still many yet to be explored.

As any reader can tell from the forgoing, we agree fully with Henry Miller. "One's destination is never a place, but a new way of seeing things." Our eyes have opened wider, our other senses have become more acute, and our minds have become more accepting with every stop on our odyssey. That ability to adopt and adapt helped humans to populate the world. Now, it helps us to learn from the populations scattered around the world. It helps us to remember that we are all citizens of the same sphere. That is a lesson that bears repeating as often as possible. And it will be repeated so long as the journey continues.

While travel will remain an integral part of our life for the next couple of decades, we are often asked, "What do you do after retirement?" To those who are curious to know, we are also immersing ourselves in various other activities, including but not limited to: expanding our childcare education business from the Asia Pacific region to North America, exploring and participating in community projects globally, and diving deeper into spirituality to find the answer to the million dollar question, "Who am I?" Above all else, we will be sharing our experiences with our grandkids, the ones who will write new pages to this book when their time comes.

As Robert Frost said in one of his early poems, "Stopping by Woods on a Snowy Evening":

> The woods are lovely, dark and deep.
> But I have promises to keep,
> And miles to go before I sleep
> And miles to go before I sleep.

And in Chanakya Niti (Chanakya's Policy) one of the verses in Sanskrit testifies to our philosophy:

गते शोको न कर्तव्यो भविष्यं नैव चिंतयेत्।
वर्तमानेन कालेन वर्तयंति विचक्षण

One should not regret the past nor worry about the future.
Wise men act in the present.

2006 Annual Holiday Letter

"The future depends on what we do in the present."
- Mahatma Gandhi

Dear Family,

As they say, life is what happens to you while you are busy making other plans. Yes, 2006 is coming to a close and we just wanted to share all the ups and downs of the year that just passed!

Varun started his final year of university and is currently going through the recruiting process to find a job after graduation. He had a great internship with Accenture in Chicago over the summer and is contemplating joining them full-time. Also, in his free time, Varun took up golf this summer and spent time with his Dad on weekends as they both worked on their swings.

Megha has been very busy with her MBA studies but has found time to enjoy life as well. She traveled to Costa Rica in March and learned to surf which was an exhilarating experience. She also led a trip of first year MBA students to Ecuador and the Galapagos Islands in August. Megha spent her summer working in Chicago at the Wrigley Company and now has a lifetime supply of gum! She is looking forward to her winter break as she learns to ski in Colorado and prepares for her study abroad next quarter (Jan-Mar 2007) in St. Gallen, Switzerland. Is this school or a long vacation? ☺

Kumud has had a busy year as well which started with a wonderful trip to India to visit her mother, family, and friends. During the year, she hit a few rough patches and underwent two surgeries - she is recovering slowly from her recent back surgery. She is in high spirits though and excited about the Christmas holidays and looking forward to spending quality time surrounded by family and friends in LA and Vegas.

Viney has had a very fulfilling year as he got promoted to Senior Executive at Accenture after spending eight years with the firm - along with the promotion, of course, comes more responsibility and more travel but he is enjoying it thoroughly! On the health front, he made a commitment to lose 15 lbs by Dec 2006 - we'll see how that goes. He seems to be on the right track though -- keep going young man!

During the 2006 Christmas season, the entire family is looking forward to spending a week in LA with friends. This is a mini reunion -- we had our big reunion on a Masala Cruise during the summer where we celebrated our friends' 25th wedding anniversary. It was a ball that will need an 'encore' for any and every reason! Life is really short and these experiences are the ones that add value and satisfaction.

In closing, we would like to wish your family happiness, peace, love, and above all sound health. May you have a wonderful holiday season - God bless!

| Viney | Kumud | Megha | Varun |
| vkmvfour@gmail.com | kumudsk@gmail.com | meghaks@hotmail.com | varunk84@hotmail.com |

Kaushal Family, 1512 Eric Lane Libertyville, IL 60048, USA
Tel: 847-367-9697 • Email: vkmvfour@gmail.com

208

Copy of Letter Sent to President Saddam Hussein in 1988

Date: 19.09.1988

To: His Excellency President Saddam Hussain

        President of Republic of Iraq

        Baghdad, Iraq

Subject: Request for a Favour for our son who was born in Iraq

Your Excellency President Saddam Hussain,

      My name is Viney Kaushal and I am currently working in Riyadh Saudi Arabia since September 1985 onwards with Bouygues, a French company. Before that, I worked in Iraq from December 1981 to August 1985 for Dragages et Travaux Publics (DTP), a French international construction company and lived with my family in Shomeli, near Hilla, Babylon.

      During our stay in Iraq, our son was born on September 19, 1984 in Diwaniya Hospital. Although we are Hindus from India, we gave him your name and that is his identity now. His name is Saddam Kaushal. The reason we gave him your name was due to your strong leadership and keeping the country united. Also, you showed great courage fighting Iranians under Khomeini for Iraqi rights from 1980 to 1988. We are very proud to give him the name of a brave leader of modern times.

      Our son who is five years old today has asked us if he can have an opportunity to see the great brave man whose name he has been given. I am therefore making a humble request to grant our son and the family audience with you in the near future at your convenience. We are sure our son will be as proud as we parents will be to meet with you and he will truly understand the significance of his name.

      Kindly oblige us with a response and confirm when we could make the visit to Baghdad to meet Your Excellency.

Yours Faithfully,

Viney Kaushal

Riyadh - Saudi Arabia

Family: Kumud Kaushal (Wife), Megha Kaushal (Daughter), Saddam Kaushal (Son)

Canadian Immigration Document

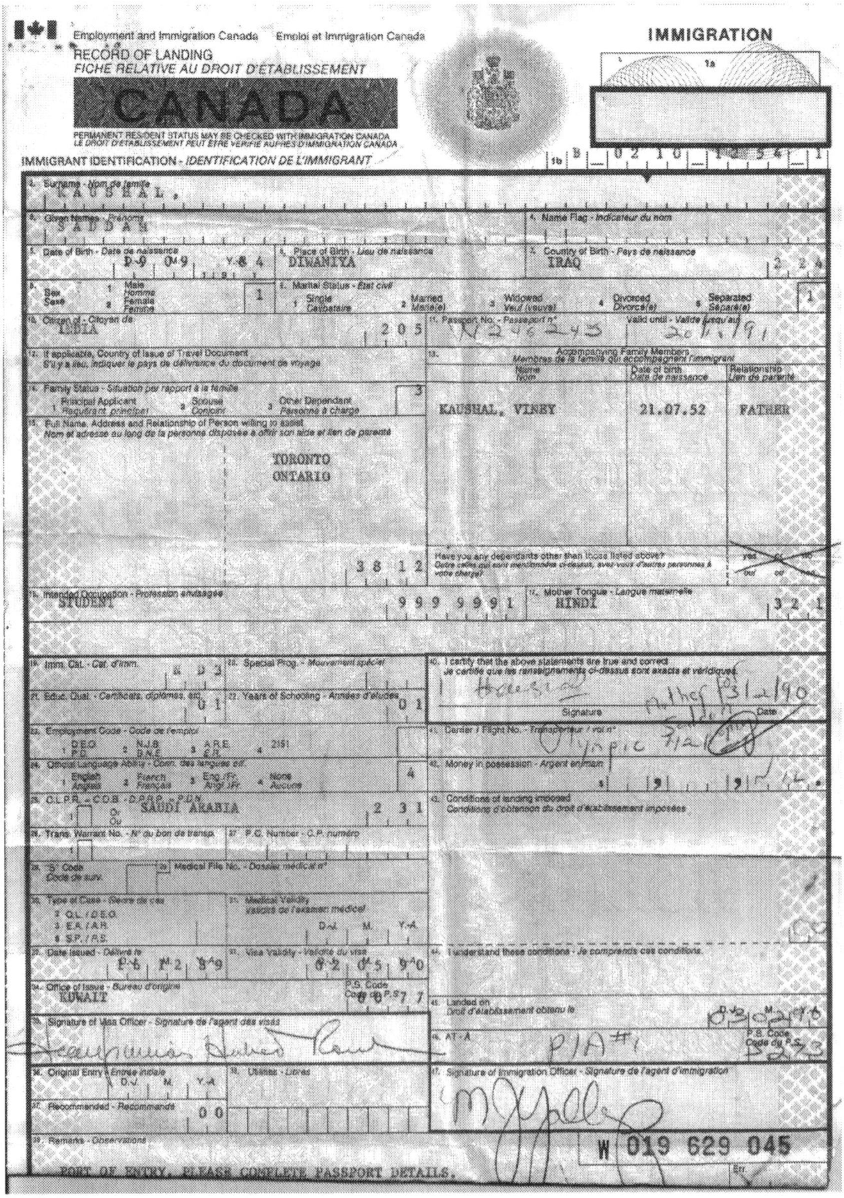

Employment and Immigration Canada Emploi et Immigration Canada

IMMIGRATION

RECORD OF LANDING
FICHE RELATIVE AU DROIT D'ÉTABLISSEMENT

CANADA

PERMANENT RESIDENT STATUS MAY BE CHECKED WITH IMMIGRATION CANADA
LE DROIT D'ÉTABLISSEMENT PEUT ÊTRE VÉRIFIÉ AUPRÈS D'IMMIGRATION CANADA

IMMIGRANT IDENTIFICATION - IDENTIFICATION DE L'IMMIGRANT

Surname - Nom de famille: KAUSHAL,

Given Names - Prénoms: SAUDAN

Name Flag - Indicateur du nom

Date of Birth - Date de naissance: D 09 M 09 Y 84

Place of Birth - Lieu de naissance: DIWANIYA

Country of Birth - Pays de naissance: IRAQ 224

Sex - Sexe: 1 Male - Homme; 2 Female - Femme: 1

Marital Status - État civil: 1 Single - Célibataire; 2 Married - Marié(e); 3 Widowed - Veuf (veuve); 4 Divorced - Divorcé(e); 5 Separated - Séparé(e): 1

Citizen of - Citoyen de: INDIA 205

Passport No. - Passeport n°: N246245

Valid until - Valide jusqu'au: 20.1.91

If applicable, Country of Issue of Travel Document
S'il y a lieu, indiquer le pays de délivrance du document de voyage

Accompanying Family Members - Membres de la famille qui accompagnent l'immigrant

Name - Nom	Date of birth - Date de naissance	Relationship - Lien de parenté
KAUSHAL, VINEY	21.07.52	FATHER

Family Status - Situation par rapport à la famille: 1 Principal Applicant - Requérant principal; 2 Spouse - Conjoint; 3 Other Dependant - Personne à charge: 3

Full Name, Address and Relationship of Person willing to assist
Nom et adresse au long de la personne disposée à offrir son aide et lien de parenté

TORONTO
ONTARIO

3812

Have you any dependants other than those listed above?
Outre celles qui sont mentionnées ci-dessus, avez-vous d'autres personnes à votre charge?

Intended Occupation - Profession envisagée: STUDENT 999 9991

Mother Tongue - Langue maternelle: HINDI 321

Imm. Cat. - Cat. d'imm.: N D 3

Special Prog. - Mouvement spécial

I certify that the above statements are true and correct.
Je certifie que les renseignements ci-dessus sont exacts et véridiques.

Signature / Date: 31/2/90

Educ. Qual. - Certificats, diplômes, etc.: 01

Years of Schooling - Années d'études: 01

Employment Code - Code de l'emploi: 1 D.E.O. P.D.; 2 N.J.B. B.N.E.; 3 A.R.E. E.R.; 4 2151

Carrier / Flight No. - Transporteur / vol n°: Olympic

Official Language Ability - Conn. des langues off.: 1 English - Anglais; 2 French - Français; 3 Eng./Fr. - Angl./Fr.; 4 None - Aucune: 4

Money in possession - Argent en main

C.L.P.R. - C.O.B. - D.P.R.P. - P.U.N.: SAUDI ARABIA 231

Conditions of landing imposed
Conditions d'obtention du droit d'établissement imposées

Trans. Warrant No. - N° du bon de transp.

P.C. Number - C.P. numéro

"S" Code - Code de surv.

Medical File No. - Dossier médical n°

Type of Case - Genre de cas: 2 C.L./D.E.O.; 3 E.R./A.R.; 4 S.P./P.S.

Medical Validity - Validité de l'examen médical: D-J M Y-A

Date Issued - Délivré le: 16 12 89

Visa Validity - Validité du visa: 02 05 90

I understand these conditions - Je comprends ces conditions.

Office of Issue - Bureau d'origine: KUWAIT

P.S. Code - Code du P.S.: 0077

Landed on - Droit d'établissement obtenu le: D-J 03 M 02 Y-A 90

Signature of Visa Officer - Signature de l'agent des visas

AT - A: PIA #1

P.S. Code - Code du P.S.

Original Entry - Entrée initiale: D-J M Y-A

Utilities - Libres

Signature of Immigration Officer - Signature de l'agent d'immigration

Recommended - Recommandé: 00

Remarks - Observations

W 019 629 045

PORT OF ENTRY, PLEASE COMPLETE PASSPORT DETAILS.

Newspaper Advertisement for Viney's First Job in Canada

JR. HUMAN RESOURCES/
PAYROLL CLERK
A growing manufacturing company in Concord (Hwy. 7 &
Keele) requires a person to prepare the weekly computerized
payroll and some basic human
resources functions. Full benefits. remuneration according to
exper. Call Angela 669-5230.

Viney's First Job

In Canada

Toronto, March 1990

Singaporean Immigration Document

Note the Warning
"Death for Drug Traffickers under Singapore Law."

Chicago Millennium Park
Summer 2014

MS Computer Science –
University of Chicago
With Varun - June 2014

Kaushal Clan during Family Wedding
Chandigarh, India March 2012

Family Picture during a wedding
LA – Aug 2012

Family Picture during a wedding
Toronto – May 2015

Vihaan and Arvin – our Grandchildren
They will carry the learnings further

Authors' Biographies

Viney Kaushal left his comfortable senior government job in India in 1981 at the age of 29 to search for greener pastures in life. In the next 34 years, this village boy moved 20 times internationally, lived in 6 countries and visited 37 countries on 5 continents, and learned continuously about cultures and people along the less-traveled roads. A double MBA, this former Managing Director of Accenture lives with his wife in Chicago, where he wants to make the best of his recent retirement. He hopes to discover as many of the remaining countries of the world as possible before the call comes.

Kumud Kaushal is an educator, banker, and entrepreneur. She left her banking career in India in 1982 to venture overseas with her husband. She grew up in India, lived in difficult places for women like Iraq and Saudi Arabia for eight years, blossomed in the free societies of Canada and the USA, and explored fifteen Asia Pacific countries extensively during her husband's posting to Singapore. She now looks forward to exploring much more of the world with her husband while enjoying her two young grandchildren in Boston. She has the distinction of having been mistaken as a local in most of the countries she has visited, especially in Asia Pacific.

Made in the USA
Lexington, KY
25 April 2016